Scarecrow
37
Library
Administration
Series
No. 10

The Library Administration Series

Lowell A. Martin, General Editor

Marketing and Public Relations for Libraries

Cosette Kies

The Library Administration Series

The Scarecrow Press, Inc.
Lanham, Maryland, and Oxford

SCARECROW PRESS, INC.

Published in the United States of America
by Scarecrow Press, Inc.
A Member of the Rowman & Littlefield Publishing Group
4720 Boston Way, Lanham, Maryland 20706
www.scarecrowpress.com

12 Hid's Copse Road
Cumnor Hill, Oxford OX2 9JJ, England

Copyright © 1987 by Cosette Kies
First paperback edition 2003

British Library Cataloguing in Publication Information Available

The hardback edition of this book was previously cataloged by the Library of
Congress as follows:

Kies, Cosette N., 1936-
    Marketing and public relations for libraries.
    (Scarecrow library administration series ; no. 10)
    Bibliography: p.
    Includes index.
    1. Public relations—Libraries.   2. Library administration.
    I. Title.   II. Series.
Z716.3K52   1987   021.7   86-20219
ISBN 0-8108-1925-2

ISBN: 0-8108-4656-X   (paper)

CONTENTS

ACRONYMS AND ABBREVIATIONS

AASL	American Association of School Librarians
ALA	American Library Association
ARL	Association of Research Libraries
BCPL	Baltimore County Public Library
CATV	Cable Television
CPL	Chicago Public Library
FOLUSA	Friends of Libraries / USA
LAMA	Library Administration and Management Association
NBC	National Book Committee
NLW	National Library Week
PIO/ALA	Public Information Office / American Library Association
PSA	Public Service Announcement (radio and television)
WHCLIS	White House Conference on Library and Information Services
WHCLIST	Task Force of WHCLIS

LIST OF FIGURES

PREFACE

WHY SHOULD *as worthy an institution as the library have to resort to marketing and public relations? Won't relevant collections and skilled personal service attract users and maintain the agency's image? And is it not somehow beneath the dignity of a profession to engage in these commercial tactics?*

Cosette Kies does not present marketing and public relations as gimmicks or as devices to manipulate the public. Rather, relations with constituency and users are shown to be integral parts of the administrative process, essential to all steps from planning to evaluation. The library that does not maintain communication with its public will not know what services to provide, will not get full use of what it does maintain, and will not know how well it is performing. Neglect of this aspect of administration will come home to the library director at budget time.

Dr. Kies applies this principle to the full range of marketing and public-relations techniques. Everything is covered, from logos to annual reports, from posters to booklists, from letterheads to exhibits, from Friends groups to fund raising. She considers not only when to use the various methods but also how to use them. Applications are made to and examples drawn from all types of libraries, public, academic, school, and special.

The joint treatment of marketing and public relations is notable. Marketing is presented as the broader, more inclusive concept. With this emphasis, topics not usually included under public relations are dealt with, such as attitude surveys, posi-

tioning of institutions, product life cycles, and merchandising. Publicity as such is fitted into this broader concept.

Almost every decision within a library has public-relations implications, whether the selection of a book, the classification assigned to it, or the loan period allowed for it. This volume advocates placing responsibility for marketing and public relations in a single person or office, but at the same time urges every member of a library staff to think of the impact on the user and on the agency's image in everything they do.

Dr. Kies is particularly qualified to make this presentation. The holder of both a Master's degree (University of Wisconsin) and a doctorate (Columbia University) in the library field, she has been an art teacher and a consultant in public relations. She has had senior responsibility both in a public library (Assistant Director, Ferguson Library, Stamford, Connecticut) and an academic library (Senior Assistant Librarian, University of Nebraska). At an earlier stage she was a children's librarian. Dr. Kies then went on to library-school instruction, first at George Peabody College and now as Chair and Professor of the library-education program at Northern Illinois University. Her special interest has been in public relations, and here we get the benefit of her skill and insight.

The present volume is the sixth in a projected series of ten on Library Administration. It takes its place beside the others in the series, and in a sense cuts across them for it deals with a concept that affects organization and finance and personnel and even library buildings.

Lowell A. Martin
Series Editor

MARKETING AND PUBLIC RELATIONS FOR LIBRARIES

1 MARKETING AND PUBLIC RELATIONS: THE DEFINITION

MARKETING and public relations [PR] are integral functions in all organizations, including libraries, although they may not be recognized as such or utilized to their fullest extent. In some cases they may not be properly understood, with consequent misuse and/or unpredictable results. Use of marketing and PR in a knowledgeable way enables librarians to take advantage of some of the most important functions of library management.

In recent years there has been more interest in marketing than in public relations for libraries. This is due partly because marketing seems new and, therefore, a possible answer to a wide assortment of management and organizational ills. Looking at the world of business and corporations, however, marketing seems to have become a dominant, dynamic, rapidly changing and developing function, while public relations has been clarified as a specific function with limited controls and powers. This is not to say that public relations should be discarded in favor of marketing in library organizations, only that the function and role of each, separately and in relationship to each other, need to be understood. They can then be used appropriately within each specific library setting.

Because of their evolution from such related fields as advertising and promotion, both public relations and marketing have suffered in public and professional repute. As later examination of the literature will show, librarians have not wholeheartedly adopted the principles of simple promotion for the good of their libraries, not to mention use of public relations

3

and/or marketing programs as a basic part of library administration. There has been widespread skepticism, suspicion
and scorn and many have regarded these activities as somehow
beneath the dignity of librarians. Some seem to believe that
libraries do not need to be touted in any special way because
their innate goodness should somehow be obvious to all.

In actual practice, these detractors and decriers of marketing
and PR generally do use these basic functions. One device is to
bury the various aspects of marketing or PR in other operations
of the organization. For example, the publication of a report
could be viewed as a management function, while response to
complaints might be viewed as part of public services. Another
tactic is simply to call marketing and PR something else, something apparently less offensive. Community relations is a term
commonly employed in some service-oriented organizations.
A number of librarians have used both these techniques in
avoiding the admission that they use marketing or PR: they
combine the two techniques described above, splitting the
basic function into pieces and also calling it something else.
Another approach of this kind is to take the surveying of public
opinion into a planning and development office and call it the
"measurement of existing attitudes." Still another common
practice is to remove some of the marketing and PR functions
from the basic operations of the library and center them in an
auxiliary group, such as a Friends organization.

Not everyone who employs such tactics is attempting to
deny the existence of marketing and PR; there may be other
reasons for using some of the techniques described above.
There are, however, librarians who do feel more comfortable
personally if they avoid any direct acknowledgment or use of
PR and marketing. By properly understanding and using public
relations and marketing, however, librarians can better learn
about their own organizations and the larger communities
which their libraries serve.

Definition of Public Relations

Contemporary definitions of public relations stress its reliance
upon two-way communication and its role as a management

responsibility. As such, PR can be simply defined as the function by which organizations, including libraries and media centers, establish and maintain open, two-way communication between the organization and its various publics. Public relations is usually specified as a function of management. The two-way communication feature can be further described as a data gathering, diagnostic, planning and evaluative technique. A more detailed definition by Rex F. Harlow, as quoted on the back of a series of pamphlets published by the National Communication Council for Human Services, Inc., which was consolidated with the Public Relations Society of America in 1977, described public relations as:

> [A] distinctive management function which helps establish and maintain mutual lines of communication, understanding, acceptance and cooperation between an organization and its publics; involves the management of problems or issues; helps management to keep informed on and responsive to public opinion; defines and emphasizes the responsibility of management to serve the public interest; helps management keep abreast of and effectively utilize change, serving as an early warning system to help anticipate trends; and uses research and sound and ethical communication techniques as its principal tools.[1]

One of the problems with defining public relations is the wide scope of the term. Because of the rather sweeping nature of a definition like Harlow's, it is not uncommon for individuals to focus on just one aspect of PR and to regard that as representing the entire PR function. One of the most common misconceptions about public relations (and marketing, too) is to concentrate on its use of promotion techniques and thus see PR simply as a synonym for promotion and publicity, or even worse, advertising. In reality, of course, public relations involves much more; it is a complicated field related to a number of other areas, including not only publicity and promotion, but also psychology, community analysis, sociology, communication theory and interpersonal relations. PR's close association with and use of techniques borrowed and adapted from these other fields has also contributed to the confusion over its meaning.

Another common misconception regarding public relations is to see it not as a distinctive aspect of management but as an exclusive function of management. To so pigeon-hole PR into the realm of management alone denies its importance as a necessary concern for all individuals within an organization, not just managers. Recognition of this broader involvement is especially important in such public-service, nonprofit institutions as libraries. An organization's formal program of planned public relations is indeed primarily a management function, but all of the organization's employees, not only the management level, need to be concerned and involved in the overall public relations of the organization.

The Definition of Marketing

A number of good, succinct definitions have been coined to describe the meaning of marketing. According to management expert Peter Drucker, the purpose of marketing is to make selling unnecessary. The aim is to know and understand the customers so well that the product or service sells itself.[2] Another definition, this time from Philip Kotler's *Principles of Marketing*, states that "marketing is human activity directed at satisfying needs and wants through exchange processes."[3] These definitions, though direct and simple, can perhaps be encapsulated in the long-time slogan of Marshall Field's, a department store noted for its quality: "Give the lady what she wants."

An obvious difference in the definition of marketing from that of public relations is in the emphasis on exchange. In the commercial world, in most cases this means the trading of money for a product or service, the process by which an individual is willing to exchange money (or barter other objects, agree to labor, etc.) for something someone else has. This type of marketing is most often associated with product marketing or the selling of a service. It describes a specific item or service which an individual is willing to purchase. Other types of marketing, however, exist and need to be considered in our examination of marketing as applied to libraries.

One type is organizational marketing. According to Philip Kotler:

> Organizational marketing is similar to this definition of public relations: the management function that evaluates public attitudes, identifies the policies and procedures of an individual or an organization with the public interest, and plans and executes a program of action to earn public understanding and acceptance.[4]

This interesting definition is somewhat different from those cited earlier for public relations. The subtle change is the phrase, "identifies the policies and procedures of an individual or an organization with the public interest." Other definitions of public relations do not include the need to align organizational policies and procedures with the public interest; emphasis is often placed on two-way communication, which may imply such alignment, but does not require it.

Another type of marketing is service marketing, which is generally applied to commercial services such as dry cleaning, automobile repair, travel arrangements, and even baby-sitting. It may also be applied to entertainment, sports, and cultural events. Although librarians might argue that libraries provide a service and should therefore utilize service marketing as a logical application, in practice most service marketing exists within the commercial world. Some services requiring special payment in libraries, such as online searches, could indeed fit into this category, but for the most part other types of marketing are more applicable to libraries.

The type of marketing which has received the most scrutiny from librarians is nonprofit marketing. Philip Kotler, author of the most-cited text in this area, defines nonprofit marketing as:

> [T]he analysis, planning, implementation, and control of carefully formulated programs designed to bring about voluntary exchanges of values with target markets for the purpose of achieving organizational objectives. It relies heavily on designing the organization's offering in terms of the target markets' needs and desires, and on using effective pricing communication, and distribution to inform, motivate, and service the markets.[5]

Nonprofit marketing seems to relate to the definitions of organizational marketing and of PR in its stress on needs, communication, and various publics. It would also seem to come closer to a definition of marketing that can be applied positively and constructively to libraries.

One further type of marketing, which needs to be considered before arriving at a definition for marketing in libraries, is social marketing.[6] This type of marketing is applied to campaigns devised to change attitudes and/or behavior in target audiences. Such campaigns have been employed to encourage the cessation of littering and smoking. They are generally not conducted for profit, but are carried out for the public good. They market an idea rather than a product. We might say that some librarians employ social marketing in their efforts to make new registrants into regular library users. Certainly, we encourage reading and information as means of escape, enrichment, self- and directed education, life improvement, and coping, and to satisfy immediate information needs. Perhaps we could be more honest in delineating our libraries' goals and objectives. It may well be that some libraries should emphasize social marketing rather than nonprofit or organizational marketing and/or PR.

PR and Marketing in the Commercial World

An examination of the basic concepts of marketing and PR and their use in the business world provides a historical context and enables us to see more clearly how those functions evolved to their present state. We can see the shifting changes in practice, how these functions are viewed today in the commercial world, and how we can understand and apply appropriate aspects to library practices.

Marketing has been a part of commerce since the beginning of business. It is, and always has been, a basic part of the process of buying and selling. The basic concept held today by ethical professionals is that marketing is a part of the process by which public needs are identified, products and services are developed to meet those needs, and the needed product or service is exchanged for a determined price.

We might think of marketing for libraries, then, as a dynamic function which identifies the needs of users and potential users, and the attendant activities by which the library meets these needs and communicates these activities to its public.

Public Relations

Public relations, although it has its roots in a number of basic human endeavors including advertising, communication, and interpersonal relations, is a product of the twentieth century. The birth of public relations as a discipline was prompted by a realization on the part of American business moguls that public opinion did indeed have an effect on their businesses. Previous attitudes on the part of these businessmen had reflected the commonly quoted, "The public be damned!" They felt that their businesses were their own and that there was no need to inform the public of their basic philosophies and practices. There was little or no acceptance of the idea that because people paid for a product or service, they had a right to be informed about the business supplying that product or service. By 1906, however, public antagonism toward some businesses had become so strong that the first publicity advisor, Ivy L. Lee, was hired by a group of anthracite coal operators who had received much negative press during labor disputes. Lee was to serve as a liaison between the anthracite operators and the press, and ultimately, the public. He stated:

> This is not a secret press bureau. All our work is done in the open. We aim to supply news. This is not an advertising agency. . . . In brief, our plan, is, frankly and openly, on behalf of business concerns and public institutions, to supply the press and public of the United States prompt and accurate information concerning subjects which it is of value and interest to the public to know about.[7]

Lee did not use the term public relations as such in describing his work until much later, but he is considered the originator of PR. The first clear definition and explanation of PR in its present sense was given by Edward Bernays in his *Crystallizing Public Opinion*, published in 1923.[8]

Although public relations was formulated to improve the image of business with the public, there continues to be widespread public distrust of business and its practitioners. Indeed, an analysis of television programs and public opinion regarding the various types of characters shown on television indicated that the majority of people in the U.S. view businessmen as evil people, and "that big businessmen are the worst of all."[9] A more recent survey in 1985 showed that 55 per cent of Americans polled believed that most corporation executives are dishonest.[10]

A similarly ironic tale could be told of the uses of PR by the U.S. government. Government use of propaganda in times of war and national stress seems to be accepted, but use of PR at other times is often viewed with distrust. Although the government may request public feedback, many individuals view such requests in a cynical, or even hostile, light.

Today, the sphere of public relations has diminished somewhat in the business world. It is now viewed as a component within a larger marketing function. Although those types of marketing most suitable for library use, such as organizational and social marketing, may seem synonymous and on a par with public relations, in the commercial world marketing is viewed as the dominant function. The value of both functions is recognized, but marketing is seen as the function which produces the desired bottom line result: profit; hence its importance. By using public relations techniques within the larger marketing framework, business experts are able to create and maintain a functional flow which identifies customer need, product (or service) development, and selling. This process is most complex and will be examined in a later chapter.

Related Definitions

Other terms should be considered in addition to library PR and marketing. In some cases these are terms representing sub-functions or components of PR and marketing processes; in other cases the terms may be related. General confusion about the exact meaning of these terms has led to considerable misuse of them. The result has been further misunderstanding regarding the definition and nature of public relations and marketing.

Communication is unquestionably a large part of the PR and marketing process. It is an activity which has been a basic part of human relationships throughout history. The well-known process of communication involving the sender, the message, and the receiver has been studied extensively, particularly in view of advances in modern technological, sociological, and psychological thought. An inseparable part of the human condition, communication is involved with PR and marketing in its sending of messages to individuals and various publics, as well as in inviting feedback. Communication may take place through the mass-media format or in smaller, more intimate, interpersonal ways.

Advertising, which is mass, paid communication, "has three functions: to inform, to persuade, and to remind."[11] It is used primarily by commercial, profit-making organizations chiefly for telling people where certain items, or services, may be purchased and why they should want to purchase them. This obvious form of commercial communication was recognized early, and was used by merchants in both verbal and graphic forms. Wall advertisements were known to exist in ancient Rome, and medieval European shopkeepers displayed signs employing symbols of their wares. Broadsides and posters were used increasingly, particularly with the invention of printing and the slowly improving literacy rate of the general public. By the seventeenth century in western Europe, posters were used to such an extent that the French government passed an edict in 1635 prohibiting their production and posting without permission.[12] The edict was, no doubt, inspired more by censorship motives than by aesthetic concerns, but the fact that such a measure was deemed necessary illustrates the increasing power of the written word. In the twentieth century the use of electronic media, particularly radio and television, has produced new styles and formats in advertising campaigns. Advertising uses whatever means are available to sell products and/or services.

Publicity specialists, sometimes called press agents in earlier days and whose role today seems limited to the almost desperate promotion of individuals who will pay for this purpose, are often former newspaper reporters who use their expertise and knowledge about newspapers and public reaction to generate publicity. Press agents also develop paid advertisements for their employers and clients, although their chief role is to make information seem exciting enough to be distributed and/or aired as news. Probably the best known user of press agentry was P. T. Barnum, whose often quoted dictum, "There's a sucker born every minute," exemplifies the prevailing attitude toward the general public prior to the twentieth century.

Publicity differs today from advertising in that in the practice of advertising, "the client pays both the advertising agency and the medium in which the advertisement is to be placed. In publicity, the client pays only the publicist."[13] An advertiser pays for space (or time with broadcasting media), and a publicist creates news and/or generates interest in the client's product or activity which is reported free of charge by the mass communications media.

Promotion differs subtly from advertising and publicity in its emphasis upon changing public attitudes, or, in other words, raising opinion regarding a product, service, organization, or individual. Publicizing and advertising create attention and remind the public of something or someone; promoting seeks to influence existing attitudes about something or someone. In modern practice, these three activities are often intertwined. Promotion, already related to advertising and publicity, is closely associated with social marketing concepts, commercial brand loyalty, and positioning principles. An example of the latter is the attempt of certain foreign sparkling water sellers to convince potential buyers that their brand is superior. Current practice in marketing is to use the term promotion to cover a number of publicity activities.

Propaganda, another aspect of the above-mentioned terms

and one of the oldest activities, is a sociological phenomenon dealing with the formation and changing of large groups' attitudes and opinions. The term is associated in most people's minds with such events as the hypnotic speeches of Hitler or the inflammatory broadsides often circulated during times of political upheaval. It is usually viewed as primarily a political technique or, at the very least, a technique to sway public opinion in order to affect political action. Certainly it is seen as the most deliberately and blatantly manipulative of all the activities under discussion here.

Community relations is a term which has been favored in the past few decades by government-associated agencies, including many public libraries, and it still has its adherents today. Occasionally called community services, this aspect of PR in business (particularly in large corporations) is generally concerned with the image of the business in the community at large. As part of this activity, a large corporation will reward its employees for being active in community affairs and will provide services and money for various community projects. The term is also used as a euphemism for PR in government and nonprofit organizations, the feeling being that the term is softer and does not carry the negative connotations of hard sell associated with public relations and marketing.

Hype is a typical Madison Avenue buzz phrase. The word became popular in the mid-1970s and describes an extreme publicity build-up. There is a difference of opinion over whether the term is an abbreviation for hyperbole, or slang to denote the high received from injecting drugs with a hypodermic needle.[14] Hype is promotion which builds on public interest.

It can be seen from the various definitions considered in this chapter that public relations and marketing are volatile words, with gradually, or sometimes quickly, changing meanings. Certainly, the terms reflect attitudes about them as functions, as well as thoughts about related activities. Just this simple examination of what the terms actually mean is illustrative of the many questions which arise in their understanding and use.

References

1. Rex F. Harlow. "Building a Public Relations Definition," *Public Relations Review* 2 (Winter 1976): 34–42.

2. Peter F. Drucker. *Management: Tasks, Responsibilities, Practices.* New York, Harper and Row, 1973, pp. 64–65.

3. Philip Kotler. *Principles of Marketing.* 2d ed. Englewood Cliffs, N.J., Prentice-Hall, 1983, p. 6.

4. *Ibid.*, p. 597.

5. Philip Kotler. *Marketing for Nonprofit Organizations.* 2d ed. Englewood Cliffs, N.J., Prentice-Hall, 1982, p. 6.

6. In an article reviewing social marketing during its first ten years as a separate marketing field, Karen Fox and Philip Kotler deplore the confusion over the definition of the term in its earlier years, sometimes used to describe marketing's social responsibilities to society rather than the marketing of social ideas. (Karen F. A. Fox and Philip Kotler. "The Marketing of Social Causes: The First 10 Years," *Journal of Marketing* 44 (Fall 1980): 25.

7. Sherman Morse. "An Awakening in Wall Street," *American Magazine* 62 (September 1906): 460.

8. Edward L. Bernays. *Crystallizing Public Opinion.* Reprint ed. New York, Liveright, 1961.

9. Ben Stein. "On TV, Businessmen Wear Black Hats," *New York Times*, 18 February 1979, p. F14.

10. Adam Clymer. "Low Marks for Executive Honesty," *New York Times*, 9 June 1985, pp. F1, 6.

11. Harvey R. Cook. *Selecting Advertising Media: a Guide for Small Business.* Washington, Small Business Administration, 1977, pp. 1, 3.

12. Ervine Metzl. *The Poster: Its History and Its Art.* New York, Watson-Guptill, 1963, p. 29.

13. Richard O'Brien. *Publicity: How to Get It.* New York, Barnes and Noble, 1977, p. 1.

14. Pierre Berton. "The Dionne Years," *New York Times Magazine,* 23 April 1978, pp. 12–15, 54–65. William Safire. "On Language," *New York Times Magazine,* 9 November 1980, p. 18.

II THE HISTORICAL DEVELOPMENT OF LIBRARY MARKETING AND PR

THE HISTORY of marketing and public relations within library circles differs little from the development of other professions' consciousness about the value of these operations. Early publicity efforts for libraries generally centered on fund-raising activities for the purchase of books and/or for library buildings. The relationship with the mass media, then primarily newspapers, is illustrated by this quotation from a recent bestseller describing the efforts of one organizer in a woman's club to strategically place influential citizens on a committee to found a library for the town: ". . . and Mrs. Bonner, who might persuade Mr. Bonner [editor of the local paper] to say helpful things about the proposed library in the *Torchlight*. . . ."[1] Library events then were generally treated as straight news by the mass media, and librarians have continued to use the good will of the media in this way.

It was John Cotton Dana, director of the Denver and Newark public libraries and the father of special libraries, who is generally credited with first espousing and encouraging the use of publicity to increase use and support of libraries. Through his writing and speeches he stressed the value to be derived from the open promotion of libraries, their services, programs, and potential value to all. A promotion award for libraries is now named in his honor. Dana, however, was not the only early exponent of promotion for libraries, as an examination of

17

library literature from those early years shows. Examples of promotion and publicity can be found, such as the use of posters in trolleys, foreign language promotion pieces to encourage immigrants to use foreign-language book collections, reports of talks to community groups, and the like.

The Early Years of Library PR

An examination of early library literature reveals an interesting pattern in the emphasis on PR (in those days usually called advertising, and later, publicity) in libraries, and in the aspects of the craft that were of particular interest to librarians. A quick analysis of the 50-year period following the birth of library periodical literature shows these interests plainly.

In the first year, 1876 (the year in which the American Library Association [ALA] and the first professional journal for librarians, *Library Journal*, were founded), an article appeared in that journal by Samuel Swet Green, Librarian of the Worcester, Massachusetts, Free Public Library. The article dealt with personal relations between librarians and readers, and Green urged personal services of a reference and readers' advisory nature to enhance use of the library's collection. He espoused four general reasons for this practice: 1/ By gaining the respect and confidence of readers it is possible to stimulate their love of study; 2/ By finding out what books the actual users of the library need it is possible to do better book collecting; 3/ By mingling with library patrons and answering their questions it is possible to make a library popular and establish an indispensable reputation in the community; 4/ Such services emphasize that the books are for the use of all people. Green's firm conclusion is that good personal relations between the librarian and readers are indispensable.[2] This is a clear, early example of marketing thinking, based on users' interests and needs, rather than the librarian's desire to force classics on unwilling readers and build up a storehouse of the world's knowledge.

By the following year, 1877, a forerunner of the helpful

publicity ideas that can be found today in library literature was a note mentioning the use in Leeds, England, of 50 transparent labels on street lamps in the vicinity of the library and its branches to advertise their locations.[3]

Nearly a decade later, 1885, a talk by Frederic B. Perkins of the San Francisco Public Library, given at the Lake George Conference, reviewed budgetary support for the nation's libraries. This article provides good insight into community support, and Perkins ends with specific recommendations aimed at increasing monetary support. He suggests, for example, the need to make the purpose of the library clear to all by not allowing use of the building for non-library purposes, such as lunching or loitering.[4]

In 1891 Samuel Swet Green, then ALA President, addressed members of the association and urged them to consider multipurpose activities in the library, and he mentioned the art gallery installed in his own Worcester, Massachusetts, public library. "The test of success of a library is its usefulness," he stated, an opinion which apparently put him at odds with Perkins over the basic purpose of public libraries.[5]

A note in *The Library Journal* in 1893 comments on the Pawtuxet Valley, Rhode Island, Library's practice of putting notices listing new books at the library in stores, post offices, and banks in the community.[6]

The argument over whether or not librarians should "lower their dignity" to advertise their libraries was referred to that same year in an address by the Principal Librarian of Liverpool to the Congress of Librarians in Chicago. He was in favor of the use of promotion and stated:

> The librarian of a public library is none the worse if he possesses some of the instincts of the commercial man, and does not view some of the popular methods of commercial people to promote trade and insure custom as beneath the dignity of an institution whose objects and aims are so high and worthy.[7]

In this last decade of the nineteenth century it was apparent that libraries were using techniques still popular today. In 1895 mention was made of a handbook for users of the Boston

Public Library,[8] and of letters sent to parents of school children from the St. Louis Public Library, urging them to send their children to the library during summer vacation.[9] John Cotton Dana, by 1896 President of ALA, exhorted the membership to "See that your library is interesting to the people of the community, the people who own it, the people who maintain it."[10]

At that same conference of ALA in Cleveland, Miss Luttie Stearns referred to the by then apparently common practice of publishing lists of books on special topics or of new books in local papers. She, too, was a firm believer in advertising:

> The Librarian who asserts that he does not believe in advertising has only to glance at the sign above his doors and the catalogs and bulletins on his counters. What are all these but advertisements of the location and contents of his library?[11]

The following year Mary Imogene Hazeltine, then Librarian of the Prendergast Free Library in Jamestown, New York, and later director of the Wisconsin library school, addressed the ALA membership in Philadelphia on the topic of "Advertising the Library" and advocated the use of booklists in newspapers, art exhibits in the library, and advertising within the library by means of displays and bulletin boards.[12]

Librarians did not advertise blindly; they were aware of the need to look at the library as an institution and to decide how to make it appealing to the public. Emma Adams, in an address to the Long Island Library Club in 1903, suggested doing away with all but absolutely necessary restrictions and urged giving community talks, providing travel and book talks and mounting exhibits in the library, viewing fiction reading as a legitimate library service, and using volunteers.

> Wherein lies the difficulty? In nine cases out of ten, I believe it lies in our having started with the wrong assumption—that the public is hungry for books. Individuals may be, but the mass of the community has no such hunger. . . . [W]e must create the hunger for books.[13]

Two years later, George Bowerman, exploring the same topic, commented that the use of bulletin boards was spreading from children's rooms to adult reading areas. He encouraged librarians to enlarge their horizons and try for feature stories in newspapers. He also suggested the economical technique of getting reprints of newspaper booklists for wider distribution in the community.[14] In the following year at the Narragansett Pier conference of ALA, Purd Wright suggested that libraries would do well to publish their own bulletins for distribution, but conceded that the cost might be prohibitive for most smaller libraries. He also stressed the need to promote things other than the books in the library, such as reading rooms and reference assistance.[15]

Advertising, though the growing trend was to call it publicity, continued to be a topic of concern to individual librarians and library associations. John Cotton Dana in 1905 reproached ALA for not founding the publicity committee "long advocated" to undertake national library publicity.[16] Eventually, the committee was indeed formed and was composed of Dana, Purd Wright, and Samuel H. Ranck.[17]

Although almost all interest in library advertising and publicity during those early years centered on public libraries, a short piece on the importance of attractive signs for libraries was written by the Acting Librarian of the University of Illinois.[18]

Throughout this period there was apparently a strong interest on the part of some librarians in advertising the library, although it was probably a controversial activity from the start. By 1911, however, the topic was apparently deemed popular enough by the publisher of John Cotton Dana's book *Modern American Library Economy* to publish the chapter on advertising as a separate pamphlet.[19]

In that same year, 1911, Samuel Ranck wrote what might be called an early how-we-did-it-good-in-our-library article. He described a highly successful program in the Grand Rapids, Michigan, Public Library involving cooperation with a local tuberculosis society which resulted in an exhibit and lecture series in the library. Thousands of individuals from the community came, with the ultimate result of improved health in Grand Rapids,[20] or so it was claimed. Also in 1911, a report by Arthur Bostwick of the subcommittee on libraries for the Social Services Conference in St. Louis brought attention to the use of library branches in St. Louis as neighborhood social centers, with club rooms provided for community groups.[21] The same year, a librarian from Toronto wrote of the importance of planning publicity in a systematic way in order to make the library's services known to all.[22]

Willis Kerr, librarian of the State Normal School, Emporia, Kansas, turned to another new field, psychology, and stressed its application to librarianship. Although much of the article deals with interpersonal relations between librarians and patrons, the underlying theme is the importance of librarians knowing their communities.[23]

An example of using commercial sponsorship to help advertise the library appeared in 1912. A note from Menominee, Michigan, told of a scheme for advertising in street cars in which merchants loaned their purchased advertising spots to the library for a week. The resulting placard advertising the library mentioned the merchant as sponsor.[24] By 1913, John Cotton Dana was pushing another approach for public librarians: serving city fathers (and controllers of the public purse) by means of municipal reference libraries.[25]

A year later another campaign began, urging ALA to employ a permanent library publicist to publicize ALA itself and to help individual librarians with promotion projects.[26] At a later session of the same ALA Council meeting in Chicago, Mary W. Plummer argued in favor of a library campaign in national, general magazines.[27]

Also in 1914, the Librarian of the Los Angeles Public Library, Everett R. Perry, stated:

> When it comes to practical methods of advertising the library's resources, we need to be constantly on the alert to discover the needs, to find fields which can be worked, and then to decide on the proper medium for accomplishing the result. Nothing can help so much to this end as an acquaintance with the community, the various sections of the town, the various classes of people, the business and industrial interests, the attitude of various individuals toward books. Several libraries have made community surveys, with highly profitable results.[28]

A stress on community relations was evident in another early how-we-did-it-good article by Miss Marion Humble, an

Instructor at the University of Wisconsin library school. She described a special issue of a local newspaper put out by the town's library board, with articles about the library, other community institutions, history, and news. The library was responsible for the content and received the profits from the sale of this special edition.[29]

Yet, this degree of sophistication was not universal in libraries (nor is it today), since other notes appeared during this period, reminding librarians not to neglect the easiest of publicity techniques, such as the need to mount a sign identifying the library, especially if it were housed in rented quarters or a private home.[30]

Small-town libraries were learning, however, and in some cases it is clear that there was a growing awareness of the need for experts upon whom local library boards could call for special campaigns when critical promotion efforts were needed. In Platteville, Wisconsin, the local board called on Miss Stearns of the state library agency for help in designing a campaign to raise money for a new library building project.[31] Statewide efforts became more noticeable during this pre-war period, also. In California the state library association sponsored a project to put a sign over every library in California saying, "Books for Everyone."[32] The effort to convince ALA to hire a publicity expert had not abated, and a report in late 1915 indicated that state associations were committed to helping in this campaign.[33]

Concern for and interest in the amount of money libraries were willing to spend on publicity became more evident. Early in 1916 a quick survey by W. H. Kerr of some typical public libraries revealed that most libraries spent less than two per cent of their budgets for publicity, whereas commercial businesses of the time were spending three to five per cent of their profits for advertising.[34]

Other statistical studies were apparently having an effect on publicity, as well. Later that year, the Edgewater, New Jersey, Public Library discovered that adult circulation did not begin to approach juvenile circulation, and posted signs in ferry-houses promoting telephone reference and other library services.[35]

Also in 1916, Joseph Wheeler, later to become well-known

for his publicity efforts as Director of the Enoch Pratt Free
Library, spoke to the Asbury Park Conference of librarians and
said, ". . . no matter how good his service, the librarian can
never hope to reach the mass of the people without his wares."[36]
In California efforts to promote libraries statewide continued. A
uniform sign (logo) for libraries was adopted and used primarily
as an identifier for library buildings throughout the state.[37]

Librarians, nevertheless, voiced the kind of concerns that
can still be heard today. A survey of Pennsylvania librarians
indicated that the majority of librarians in the state felt that
one of the greatest handicaps to their work was the indifference
of the public.[38]

Service to foreign-speaking populations was growing. In
1917, the library in Worcester, Massachusetts, printed signs in
Swedish to put in neighborhood stores informing new immigrants about Swedish-language materials in the library.[39]

Prior to U.S. entry in World War I, some activities were
emerging in American libraries which were to have considerable influence in later library development. For example, the
equivalent of storefront libraries were established in Springfield, Illinois, for both children and adults[40]; continued efforts
were made to use all available advertising means to promote
libraries[41]; and there was continued pressure to persuade ALA
to hire a full-time publicist.[42]

During the First World War, ALA and its librarians chan-
neled much activity into the war effort, with particular enthu-
siasm devoted to ALA's campaign to supply U.S. servicemen in
camps with books. The library literature of this time includes
many examples of library promotion for this effort, featuring
pleas for the citizenry to bring their books to the libraries so
that they could be sent on to soldiers in camps and overseas.
This campaign was a success, not only in meeting the basic
objective of the program but in providing a by-product in one
of the best war posters produced during that period (see Figure
1).

Activity on behalf of library promotion at home did not
cease, however, and Willis H. Kerr reported on a survey by the
ALA Publicity Committee of 3,500 public, academic and institution libraries. A report on the eight per cent return indi-

Figure 1
World War I poster designed by Charles Buckles Fall

cated that libraries still were not spending much money for publicity (large public libraries spent .0074 per cent of their budgets for publicity, average public libraries spent 1.10 per cent, small public libraries 00.7 per cent, and village libraries 00.7 per cent) and there was still resistance to the very idea of advertising:

> Publicity work, like classification, seems to us a very inexact science, in which definite results cannot usually be expected to follow. As I believe that millions are wasted annually on unnecessary and unwise advertising, so I believe that thousands may be squandered by us librarians unless we keep our heads and decline to be stampeded into this publicity vortex. At the same time I think that a "publicity agent" would be very useful in large libraries, provided she possessed common sense and did not try to supplant the librarian. [From a large eastern public library.][43]

A more sophisticated approach to promotion was encouraged by Earl Browning at the close of the war. He urged librarians to study and consider all aspects of merchandising, including a look at the overall atmosphere of the library and the need for a business approach in library advertising.[44] This article might be considered one of the first in library literature to espouse marketing principles for improved library promotion.

In 1919 a series, each perhaps a column, appeared in the *Library Journal* under the heading of "Library Publicity." It was written by Frank Stockbridge, Director of Bowker's Library Information Service. Each column explored a promotion topic, such as the necessity to gear advertising to community purse holders, who might or might not be library users.[45] In that same year Mary Imogene Hazeltine compiled a very useful two-part series outlining various techniques libraries should consider for library publicity.[46]

In 1920 one of the earliest articles urging academic librarians to use the principles of publicity appeared. The article outlined various publicity efforts to be aimed at different segments of the academic community—faculty, staff, and students.[47]

The 1920s saw the rise of a rather naïve notion among some of those who had become staunch advocates of library promotion. One article endorsing the ideas of promotion even went so far as to state, "Advertising will sell anything. . . ."[48]

Another landmark event in 1920 was the celebration of the first Children's Book Week, which has been observed ever since. Beginning as a New York-dominated event, it caught on elsewhere, and one of its best loved features was an annual poster designed by a noted illustrator of children's books.[49]

A long, three-part series of articles by Gilbert O. Ward, technical librarian of the Cleveland Public Library, which appeared in *Public Libraries*, no doubt served as a preliminary exploration of the subject of publicity planning for his book, *Publicity for Public Librarians*, published in 1924, the first full-length treatment on the subject of library publicity.

The final item from the library literature to be noted here is a proposal presented in 1924 by Willis Kerr on behalf of the Publicity Committee of ALA for a National Library Week program.[51] It is sad to realize that this idea did not become reality until the mid-1950s, and ironic that it came about because of the determination of the National Book Committee, not through ALA's efforts.

By the 1920s many articles were appearing in library publications on many diverse aspects of library publicity, including publicity for small libraries, direct mail advertising, use of billboards, local and state book and library weeks, competitions, use of a town's welcome wagon, tips for newspaper stories, displays, and other techniques. The first volume of *Library Literature*, covering the years 1921–1932, includes more than two tightly packed pages of citations under the heading of "Publicity." It is obvious that there was a growing interest and acceptance of promotion in the profession.

More Recent Years

Following these early years, articles on public relations, for such it was at long last called, appeared with regularity in most library periodicals. There were few monographs treating the subject, but some titles were published during the 1930s, '40s and '50s by individuals whose names are still familiar today, such as Marie Loizeaux and Sarah Wallace.

Critics of library promotion continued to scorn the activity. More difficult to judge are the words of some of those who were well known for their excellent practice and support of library promotion, who would include in their talks disclaimers or apologies on the topic. An example of this is the prelude to a piece by Joseph Wheeler, by then (1930) Librarian of the Enoch Pratt Free Library:

> I feel that I must explain myself in talking here on a subject which I have been attempting to leave alone for some time. Publicity is only a means to an end; one method among many. Having got out a whole book on the subject, I feel that other subjects interest me more and I do not care for being considered a "publicity hound" even in the better sense.[52]

By the late 1950s a new project sparked greater sophistication and interest in library public relations: the establishment of National Library Week by the National Book Committee in cooperation with the American Library Association. National Library Week was seen as a focus for year-round publicity efforts by libraries, and many workshops were held to teach librarians the rudiments of publicity and public relations planning and execution. Although attacked by some librarians, most often academics, as some sort of spurious activity comparable to National Pickle Week, the program provided valuable training for many and was the nucleus for a concerted effort by the profession to promote books and libraries. In 1974 the National Book Committee was dissolved, due primarily to lack of continued funding by the publishing community, and ALA picked up the National Library Week program, omitting, however, the series of training workshops for librarians.

During the most recent decade the noteworthy development in library promotion and public relations has been the increased examination of marketing as a possible vehicle for improving the library image and library use. The only danger in this transference of interest is the possibility of a total desertion of public relations, which, although somewhat dormant at present, is still valuable and useful. Later chapters will examine the principles and processes involved in both public relations and marketing, and will make clear, it is hoped, that libraries can benefit from both; it is not a matter of making a choice between the two.

References

1. Helen Hooven Santmyer. ". . . *And Ladies of the Club.*" New York, G. P. Putnam, 1982, p. 205.

2. Samuel Swet Green. "Personal Relations Between Librarians and Readers," *Library Journal* 1 (1876): 74–81.

3. *Library Journal* 1 (30 June 1877): 377.

4. Frederic B. Perkins. "Public Libraries and the Public, with Special Reference to the San Francisco Public Library," *Library Journal*, 10 (September 1885): 223–229.

5. Samuel Swet Green. "Conference of Librarians, San Francisco, October 12–16, 1891, Address of the President," *Library Journal* 16 (December 1891): 1–9.

6. "Advertising New Books," *Library Journal* 18 (May 1893): 143.

7. Peter Cowell, "How to Popularize a Free Library," *Library Journal* 18 (November 1893): 461–65.

8. *Library Journal* 20 (November 1895): 374.

9. "Library Advertising," *Library Journal*, 21 (July 1896): 327.

10. John Cotton Dana. "Conference of Librarians, Cleveland and Mackinaw. Address of the President," *Library Journal* 21 (December 1896): 1–5.

11. L. E. Stearns. "Advertising a Library," *Library Journal* 21 (December 1896): 37–40.

12. Mary Imogene Hazeltine. "Advertising a Library," *Library Journal* 22 (October 1897): 74–79.

13. Emma L. Adams. "Ways of Making a Library Useful," *Library Journal* 28 (July 1905): 286–290.

14. George F. Bowerman. "Library Advertising," *Public Libraries*, 10 (July 1905): 335–39.

15. Purd B. Wright. "Some Methods of Library Advertising," *Library Journal*, 31 (August 1906): 86–88.

16. John Cotton Dana. "What State and Local Library Associations Can Do for Library Interests," *Library Journal* 30 (September 1905): 17–21.

17. *Ibid.*

18. F. K. W. Drury. "On Making Signs," *Library Journal* 33 (August 1908): 315.

19. John Cotton Dana. "Advertising," in *Modern American Library Economy As Illustrated by the Newark Free Public Library*, by John Cotton Dana. Woodstock, Vt., Elm Tree Press, 1910.

20. Samuel H. Ranck. "The Public Library as a Factor in Civic Development," *Library Journal* 36 (March 1911): 116–121.

21. Arthur E. Bostwick. "The Social Work of the St. Louis Public Library," *Library Journal* 36 (September 1911): 461–63.

22. George E. Scroggie. "Library Publicity," *Library Journal* 36 (June 1911): 289–292.

23. Willis H. Kerr. "Psychology for Librarians," *Public Libraries* 16 (December 1911): 425–430.

24. Lois Amelia Spencer. "Advertising in Street-Cars," *Wilson Library Bulletin* 8 (July–August 1912): 133–34.

25. John Cotton Dana. "The Public Library and Publicity in Municipal Affairs," *Library Journal* 38 (April 1913): 198–201.

26. Willis H. Kerr. "Suggestions for Greater Library Publicity," *Library Journal* 39 (March 1914): 192–95.

27. *Ibid.*, pp. 194–95.

28. Everett R. Perry. "Aims and Methods of Library Publicity," *Library Journal* 39 (April 1914): 259–266.

29. Marion Humble. "The Prairie du Chien Idea," *Wisconsin Library Bulletin* 10 (April 1914): 68–70.

30. *Library Journal* 39 (May 1914): 405.

31. "The Platteville Carnegie Campaign," *Wisconsin Library Bulletin* 10 (May 1914): 98–100.

32. "Signs," *Library Journal* 40 (September 1915): 681.

33. "A Publicity Expert for Public Libraries," *Public Libraries* 20 (December 1915): 469–71.

34. W. H. Kerr. "Publicity Methods for Libraries and Library Associations," *ALA Bulletin* 10 (January 1916): 14–17.

35. *Library Journal* 41 (July 1916): 514–15.

36. Joseph Wheeler. "The Larger Publicity of the Library," *ALA Bulletin* 10 (July 1916): 175–80.

37. "County Free Library Sign Day in California," *Library Journal* 41 (October 1916): 783–84.

38. Henry F. Marx. "The Indifference of the Public to the Library," *Public Libraries* 21 (December 1916): 445–449.

39. *Library Journal* 42 (January 1917): 73.

40. *Library Journal* 43 (January 1917): 75.

41. "Publicity Measures Proposed by A.L.A. Committee," *Library Journal* 42 (April 1971): 299–301.

42. Charles H. Compton. "Adventures in Library Advertising," *Library Journal* 42 (July 1917): 515–19.

43. Willis H. Kerr. "The Gist of the A.L.A. Library Publicity Survey," *ALA Bulletin* 11 (July 1917): 130–134.

44. Earl W. Browning. "What Libraries Can Learn from Salesmanship," *New York Libraries* 6 (November 1918): 128–29.

45. Frank Parker Stockbridge. "Publicity for Libraries," *Library Journal* 44 (January, February, March, May, June, July, September, 1919): 31–32, 111–13, 171–72, 311–12, 391–93, 459–61, 596–98.

46. Mary Imogene Hazeltine. "Checklist of Library Publicity Methods," *Wisconsin Library Bulletin* 15 (April 1919): 91–93 and (May 1919): 121–25.

47. Francis K. W. Drury. "Publicity for College Libraries," *Library Journal* 45 (1 June 1920): 487–89.

48. Ray Johnson. "Selling the Library Idea," *Library Journal* 45 (1 February 1920): 105.

49. "Children's Book Week in the Libraries," *Library Journal* 45 (15 October 1920): 835–38.

50. Gilbert O. Ward. "Planning to Make the Public Library Known," *Public Libraries* 27 (February 1922): 77–80; (March 1922): 141–146, and (April 1922): 210–14.

51. Willis Kerr. "National Library Week: The Publicity Committee's Proposal," *ALA Bulletin* 16 (Papers and Proceedings of the 44th Annual Meeting of the ALA, 1924): 133.

52. Wheeler, Joseph L. "A Publicity Program." *Wilson Bulletin for Librarians* 5 (1931): 497. (A paper read at the meeting of the League of Library Commissions, December 29, 1930, at the

Appreciation is expressed to Anna Neal for her assistance in the historical sections of this chapter.

Midwinter meeting of ALA.) Wheeler was probably referring to his landmark work, *The Library and the Community* (Chicago: American Library Association, 1924), which dealt not just with publicity, but with the larger concept of community relations.

III THE PRINCIPLES OF MARKETING AND PR: BASIC CONCEPTS

CERTAIN PRINCIPLES need to be kept in mind in order to use public relations and/or marketing effectively. Some are particularly important in connection with nonprofit organizations such as libraries. An understanding of these principles helps clarify the nature of PR and marketing, and highlights some important tenets for their use.

Philip Lesly has pointed out some critical principles and trends in public relations, including:

1/ Complexity of group attitudes
2/ Emphasis on measuring intangibles
3/ Resistance of attitudes
4/ Trend away from oversimplification
5/ Awareness of fallacies about communication
6/ Changing role of the media
7/ Name as image factor
8/ Edifice as a visual symbol
9/ Evaluation of public relations
10/ Growing professionalism[1]

A common element throughout these concerns and principles is communication, in all its forms, from the mass media to various types of informal and formal communication. Included but too often forgotten is the very influential word-of-mouth type of public relations which is so important in the formation of individual and group attitudes. Also touched

35

upon are the image of an organization's name and the build-
ing(s) in which it is housed.

A number of marketing theorists have presented their basic
concepts, or principles, of marketing. Benson Shapiro suggests
that there are four essential principles:

1/ The self-interest aspect of the exchange, which neces-
sitates keeping the buyer's needs in mind
2/ The marketing task, which means attention to the
marketing process/plan/system at all times
3/ The marketing mix of product development, the
price, the promotion and distribution
4/ The distinctive competence of the organization, or
business, in offering a product to the public[2]

Here we see a different stress from the principles enumer-
ated for PR: the concern with identifying customer need. Another difference is the attention to the marketing mix (product,
package, price and placement), and a shared concern is the
need to develop an organizational image.

Another expert, Philip Kotler, reminds us that there are
more than basic marketing concepts to consider. We must
understand the differences between marketing concepts and
other related principles, such as:

1/ The production concept, which maintains the consumer's favor for products that are available and af-
fordable; hence the practicality in stressing improved
production and distribution.
2/ The product concept, which states that consumers
favor products offering superior quality, performance
and features; thus the need to make continuous product improvement.
3/ The selling concept, which holds that consumers will
not buy enough unless there is a concerted selling and
promotion effort.
4/ The marketing concept, which, in its modern form,
states that by determining target audiences' needs, the
product will sell itself.

5/ The societal marketing concept, which says that not only should the producer determine audiences' needs, but do so in a manner that enhances society's well-being.[3]

This list introduces some new notions in addition to customer need: sizing up the competition, and the need to consider societal implications. These marketing concepts are useful, but when considering PR and marketing principles it is useful to think about a number of other aspects as well. In this chapter we will examine the following principles of marketing and PR for libraries:

1/ The need to know the nature of public opinion, personal motivation and group motivation.

2/ The definition of what we are "selling," or the nature of our "product."

3/ The knowledgeable delineation of our target audiences.

4/ The decision on selecting marketing (primarily based on need) or public relations (based on two-way communication) as the prime function for the library.

5/ The importance of knowing the library's community.

6/ The need for expertise in fashioning communication/promotion messages.

7/ The active seeking and use of feedback.

8/ The use of results of evaluation to build for the future.

9/ The need for continuing evolution of PR and marketing.

10/ The importance of using PR at all times, not just in times of trouble.

11/ Clear recognition of the benefits to be derived from using PR and/or marketing.

12/ The value of using participatory management in PR and/or marketing to ensure staff understanding and involvement.

Public Opinion

Public relations and marketing involve two-way, mutual communication. In order for this to work efficiently and effectively, there must be some feeling on the part of the organization about the attitudes of the people with whom it is trying to establish and maintain two-way communication. One aspect of this phase of the operation involves the determination of these attitudes, or public opinions. Public opinion ". . . is a collection of individual opinions on an issue of public interest, and they usually note that these opinions can exercise influence over individual behavior, group behavior, and public policy."[4] Public opinion and attitudes are indispensable factors in PR and marketing. The importance of public opinion has been recognized throughout history, by Greek theorists who stressed the importance of public will and by despotic monarchs concerned about the mood of the "common rabble." This public will, which can be described rather simplistically as public opinion intensified into action, has made itself known throughout history in such dramatic events as revolutions and crusades. Consideration for public opinion seems to have surfaced primarily during times of crisis. Today we see a spate of public opinion polls during election times and a fascination with measuring public attitudes about a wide variety of subjects. Inaccurate assessment of public opinion can have devastating effects, such as the unexpectedness of the overthrow of the Iranian Shah in early 1979 and the impact of that event on the American government.

Public opinion is often ascertained by means of polls, which can survey whole populations or samples of given populations in an effort to determine attitudes. Privately operated polling companies are very active today and their findings have an impact on the public at large, as well as on those who commission the polls. An example of how these polls can measure changes in attitude is one by Gallup in the spring of 1979, which discovered that 51 per cent of the American public had confidence in newspapers, as compared with only 39 per cent in 1973.[5]

Attempts to manipulate public opinion have been categorized sometimes as propaganda. This kind of activity has been very much a part of American history. Consider the importance placed on swaying public opinion and attitudes in favor of the cause of independence during the American Revolution. During the Jacksonian era there developed the concept of the Common Man and the dominance of majority public opinion as a determining factor in forming national public policy.[6] Much in the development of America has been shaped by the formation of public opinion and its expression in public will.

Public opinion is sometimes difficult to gauge because of its temporal, or often culturally nationalistic, character. The elusive nature of public opinion and the personalized views that can be adopted about it are illustrated by the attitude of Pedro II, the last emperor of Brazil:

> He seemed to equate national opinion with national well-being and thus divorced it in his mind from public opinion, which was, according to his thought, often misguided, erroneous, and emotional, and therefore not always in accord with the best interests of the realm. It was in short the fickle whim of the masses.[7]

Changes in public opinion cannot be predicted easily, and shifts sometimes can be identified only when they are focused by a matter of strong current interest or controversy. This is the pure meaning of public opinion; it is really a group attitude regarding a particular issue. Attitudes are complex, however, and shaping each individual's attitude about an issue may be a number of underlying reasons. When a collective public opinion is sought, understanding those underlying reasons is important. They may vacillate or remain fixed, depending on the firmness of conviction involved.

One example of how difficult it can be to determine public opinion involved proposed legislation to censor sexually related materials. Librarians have traditionally supported the concept of intellectual freedom and the First Amendment, but personal and professional attitudes can conflict. During a state library association's annual conference a debate took place on whether or not to join in a lawsuit with bookstore owners to test the constitutionality of a rushed-through, emotionally charged censorship law. Some librarians hesitated at first over automatically subscribing to intellectual freedom principles because of personal religious and moral convictions, as well as strong public sentiment regarding the bill which it was thought might affect future library funding. What might have been regarded originally as easily predictable public opinion in this group became a controversial issue.

Cantril's Laws of Public Opinion

In the late 1940s Hadley Cantril published a list of fifteen principles which govern public opinion:

1/ Opinion is highly sensitive to important events.

2/ Events of unusual magnitude are likely to swing public opinion temporarily from one extreme to another. Opinion does not become stabilized until the implications of events are seen with some perspective.

3/ Opinion is generally determined more by events than by words—unless those words are themselves interpreted as "events."

4/ Verbal statements and outlines of courses of action have maximum importance when opinion is unstructured, when people are suggestible and seek some interpretation from a reliable source.

5/ By and large, public opinion does not anticipate emergencies; it only reacts to them.

6/ Psychologically, opinion is basically determined by self-interest. Events, words, or any other stimuli affect opinion only in so far as their relationship to self-interest is apparent.

7/ Opinion does not remain aroused for any long period of time unless people feel their self-interest is acutely involved or unless opinions—aroused by words—are sustained by events.

8/ Once self-interest is involved, opinions are not easily changed.

9/ When self-interest is involved, public opinion in a democracy is likely to be ahead of official policy.

10/ When an opinion is held by the slight majority or when opinion is not solidly structured, an accomplished fact tends to shift opinion in the direction of acceptance.

11/ At critical times, people become more sensitive to the adequacy of their leadership—if they have confidence in it, they are willing to assign more than usually responsible to it. If they lack confidence in it, they are less tolerant than usual.

12/ People are less reluctant to have critical decisions made by their leaders if they feel that somehow they, the people, are taking some part in the decision.

13/ People are able to form opinions more easily with respect to goals than with respect to methods necessary to reach those goals.

14/ Public opinion, like individual opinion, is colored by desire. And when opinion is based chiefly on desire rather than on information, it is likely to show especially sharp shifts with events.

15/ By and large, if people in a democracy are provided educational opportunities and ready access to information, public opinion reveals a hard-headed common sense. The more enlightened people are to the implication of events and proposals for their own self-interest, the more likely they are to agree with the more objective opinions of realistic experts.[8]

Cantril's principles are based on his research into public opinion and personal motivation. In general, they are meant to apply to large masses of the public, but they can sometimes be applied to smaller groups as well. They may appear to some to be natural, common sense statements, or to others, perhaps too highly charged with psychological motivations to be stated so simply, but they do relate to certain characteristics of public relations and marketing and should be considered when attempting to measure or form public opinion.

Personal Motivation

What forces motivate individuals to form opinions and attitudes varies from person to person. Before group public opinion can be determined with any degree of accuracy, one must understand what is involved in motivating the individuals within any group. One of the best-known, and probably most commonly accepted theories of motivation is Abraham Maslow's hierarchy of needs. This theory is based on the premise that individuals have certain needs which must be met in sequence, in order to move to the next higher need. The result might be considered a basic needs indicator or temperature gauge, showing why people behave as they do and what motivates various actions. The needs, from the lowest to the highest, are:

1/ Physical needs, including food, sleep, health, bodily needs, exercise and sex.

2/ Safety needs, including security, protection, comfort, and orderly surroundings.

3/ Love needs, including acceptance, a feeling of belonging, membership in the group, love and affection, and group participation.

4/ Self-esteem needs, including recognition, confidence and leadership, achievement and ability, competence, success, and strength and intelligence.

5/ Self-actualization needs, including self-fulfillment of potential, doing things purely for the challenge of accomplishment, intellectual curiosity and fulfillment, creativity and aesthetic appreciation, and acceptance of reality.[9]

These five levels, according to Maslow, must be pursued in order. When an individual has met the needs of one level, there is automatic progression to the next higher level. Thus, in order to encourage individuals to be motivated at level five, the level of self-actualization, the majority of needs within each of the first four levels must first be met.

Group Motivation

Individuals form into a variety of groups which exhibit many characteristics; also, each individual belongs to a variety of groups. For example, every individual can be automatically categorized according to certain demographic characteristics such as sex, age, race, economic status, nationality, educational level, and so on. Groups of this nature are sometimes called *statistical groups*. Another, and often more useful, way to group individuals for PR and marketing purposes is by function and/or common interest; these are individuals who have come together, often voluntarily, for a purpose. As a member of an *interest group* a person has *chosen* to join with other individuals; the group will have certain standards and customs, rules for behavior, and shared beliefs. Examples of interest groups include community organizations, clubs, and casual social groups. Of current interest to marketing strategists are strongly cohesive interest groups, sometimes called *reference groups*, which have many similarities with adolescent peer groups. Members of reference groups tend to have many of the same attitudes, interests, and loyalties. Attitudes on some issues may be polarized as between one reference group and another, and discussion of issues is likely to intensify the feelings of individuals within the group.[10] The influence of reference groups on the attitudes and behavior of some individuals may account in part, for example, for the drop-off rate of library use in the teenage years.

Peer pressure involves more than a group's scoffing at individual deviant choices. Involved too is approval for choices that concur with group norms. It means being "one of the gang," not being different. For some individuals, this kind of conformity is very important. If regular library use is not part of the group's behavior, then an individual in the group is less likely to use the library independently. Library use, of course, may not even rate as approved or disapproved group behavior, in which case group members may make their own determination about use of the library.

Definition of the Product

One of the most difficult areas librarians have had to deal with in public relations and marketing is the definition of what libraries are promoting. There are varying opinions within the profession as to what libraries are and should be, and this has contributed to the basic problem. There has even been difficulty in agreeing on who should make this determination, librarians or others—for example, members of the community the library serves. Because of these difficulties, libraries have had an inconsistent image, which has resulted in confusion in the general public's mind about the purpose of libraries. We have in large part created this confusion ourselves; the profession needs to agree as to what libraries are and what we should be saying about them.

There has been a problem, for example, in defining the library as an institution. Is the purpose of the library to be a storehouse of man's collective knowledge, or a place where people can get what they want? Is the library a definite place, confined by a building, or is it a concept of service which reaches out to its community in various ways? Is the library a home for fine, quality literature, or a potpourri of popular books, nonprint materials, innovative services and imaginative programs? Is it a place to educate oneself, or a place to come for information for a specific purpose? Is it there to guide individuals in self-directed learning and seeking, or only to provide information upon request? Is the library a stately, quiet place for reflective research and study, or a bright, cheerful, busy spot?

These and other questions have been argued for years in library circles, and agreement about them is not likely anytime soon. Each library has its own purpose, we can say. but how clearly do we understand that as librarians? And if we don't understand clearly ourselves, how can we shape a clear image of the library to project to the public at large? It should be no surprise, if we have no clear image of ourselves, that the public does not understand our purpose either.

Without a conviction about which image to project, it is almost impossible to shape messages to appeal to individuals and groups, telling them why they should use the library and its services. If we don't know what we're selling, we can hardly expect the public to buy.

Finally, we need to decide whether we are promoting, or selling, the library as a place to be used (social marketing), or as a place to be supported (organizational marekting) for the basic good of the community.[11] We need to admit some harsh realities: we don't know what we're promoting, and we're not sure who we're trying to sell it to. All in all, a marketer's nightmare.

Target Audiences

One of the basic practices in marketing is the identification of target audiences, or group segmentation, and the promotion of specifics to particular groups. The group is defined in a particular way and then the product is described in terms that the defined group will be interested in, and, ultimately, buy. Libraries have been interested in target audiences, or user groups, and in recent times have devoted much planning and promoting to groups rather than individuals. Some basic library services have traditionally been based on group definition—services to children, to the busness community, to students.

Segmenting may be done according to demographics (age, sex, education, income level, etc.), socioeconomic classes (income, spending habits), geographic location (urban/rural, climate, distance), and psychographic characteristics (life style, status; see Chapter 5). Other groups may be identified on the basis of interests and needs.

Certain uncontrolled variables affect the make-up of groups, however, and librarians need to be aware that in many cases groups are not static, but constantly shifting in their membership. Examples of such variables include socio-cultural trends (opera is currently "in"), economic trends (high unemployment), consumer behavior (casual running-up of debt), technological developments (home computer use, video-text), competing activities (cultural events and bookstore promotions), political and legal trends (degree of social consciousness, such as adult literacy), and distribution structural trends (why people get what they need, and where). Additional elements include such characteristics as the sophistication of the users or potential users; for example, those individuals who know what the competition is (e.g., bookstores) but still prefer to check first for needed material at the library.[12]

A wide variety of target audiences may be identified by any library, including those already using the library and those the library sees as potential users, or at least as people who should be aware of the library as a public good. Some groups can be easily identified by merely looking at the service points a particular library has established. In an academic library these might include some departmental libraries, dormitory libraries, and collections in centers used for extension classes. Another way to produce a list of target audiences is via the different services provided by a library. In a special library we might find certain services available to particular workers with special needs in a company; other services may be used primarily by one group of individuals who can easily be categorized as a segment.

An important factor in marketing segmention, however, is the knowledge that any one individual may belong to many different groups. A puzzle long contemplated by commercial marketers is how to identify common ground among a number of different groups in order to aim advertising messages to that common point, thus eliminating the need for multiple messages to a variety of groups. This is not, obviously, always effective, and one needs to consider drawbacks as advantages of this approach. For example, if a library is planning to send information through the mail to various groups, it is wise to check and avoid sending duplicate items to the same person because of his/her multiple memberships. It might be said that reinforcement never hurts, but it is more likely that the individual receiving a number of copies of the same mailing will be irritated at an increase in "junk" mail and the careless extravagance of the library in letting it happen.

According to Anne Matthews certain criteria should be applied in selecting target groups:

1/ Accessibility, or reasonable expectations of reaching the group.
2/ Focus of the group, or common interest.
3/ Viability, or suitable size of the group.
4/ Opportunity to the library to establish new programs and weed out old ones.
5/ Staff considerations, including staff expertise.
6/ Relation to other market groups, and particularly its distinctiveness from other groups.
7/ Timing, in order to meet the needs of the group.
8/ Public relations emphasis, in providing an advantage to the library.
9/ Loyalty, or increasing steady use of library.
10/ Alternatives; rationale for selecting this group over another. [13]

If a library has already decided to focus services and programs toward certain specific groups, it only makes sense to use those same groups for most promotion purposes. These likely users are the primary targets. Other groups and individuals to be informed about new programs and services are secondary targets, generally individuals who are thought of not so much as potential users, but as those who will help get the word out to others and perhaps provide support for new programs and services.

Marketing or Public Relations?

If a library is to be effective in marketing or public relations, it must understand and make a commitment to the process.

Neither process can be used to its potential without understanding how it works, what it can do, and what its limitations are. The decision to use public relations, or the broader concept of marketing (which includes public relations), is not a difficult one, once it is realized that public relations already exists in every organization, whether it has been planned or not. The pieces of the process are there and can be identified, even if they are called by different names.

The essential element in the choice of marketing or public relations, for most libraries, is whether or not the library concerned is willing to commit itself fully to fulfillment of the needs and wishes of patrons and potential patrons. In these days of tight budgets and a stress upon accountability, the library that chooses marketing must often turn away from such traditional practices of librarianship as building balanced collections or attempting to preserve the best of the world's knowledge. The choice may be made more easily if there are other libraries geographically nearby that can serve these more traditional functions. For isolated libraries serving larger geographic areas the choice can be more difficult.

Knowing the Community

It should be apparent that knowledge of the library's community is essential if one is to select target audiences skillfully. Librarians need to consider all or as many as possible of the groups in their communities when planning library collections, services, and programs.

For many decades, public librarians have been concerned to know more about their communities and interest in more precise community analysis was encouraged by ALA with a number of projects, including the Library-Community Project of the late 1950s, conducted by Ruth Warncke, who later became Deputy Director of ALA. Borrowing heavily from social scientists who developed a variety of techniques for community analysis, this approach has evolved into the public library performance measures of the 1970s. These measures are based on extensive community analysis and provide public libraries with their own individualized standards. Planning thus becomes a more precise process.

Other kinds of libraries—academic, school and special—have their own communities, not delineated by county or city boundaries as in the case of public libraries, but constructed on the basis of use as defined by some higher authority, usually the funding authority. In academic libraries the community may be only members of the university's immediate constituency, or some services and materials may be made grudgingly available to townspeople or to networks. School libraries generally provide direct services only to the students, teachers, administration and staff of their own schools or school systems. Special libraries have generally been established by an authority, such as a corporation headquarters or government agency, for specific purposes, and the community the library serves is carefully delineated.

Knowing the community involves considering many aspects, not only demographics, but socioeconomic features, lifestyles and other factors which may influence the individuals within various groups. Librarians can acquaint themselves with their communities through research and reading published information, through observation and a variety of surveying techniques, among other methods. Community analysis should be viewed, however, as an ongoing process, for communities change, and librarians who do not keep abreast of such changes may find their libraries stagnating and little used.

Communication/Promotion Techniques

One constant limitation is that there are few librarians who are specially trained in promotion techniques. In larger systems it is possible to hire specialists in marketing, public relations, journalism, and the like, but in smaller libraries librarians are faced with doing the promotion job themselves. A lack of knowledge sometimes results in hesitation, occasional blunders, and rarely (fortunately) flat-out disasters. For the most part, however, librarians have worked hard to acquire some knowledge of promotion and are eager to learn more about ways to improve the image of their libraries.

Seeking Feedback

Feedback involves three major groups from whom librarians seek reactions to collections, services, and programs: 1/ library users, 2/ individuals in the community who are potential users, and 3/ library staff members. In spite of the variety of methods used to encourage feedback, it remains a difficult process, partly because individuals do not, for one reason or another, always give honest reactions.

Some methods used for gathering feedback include suggestion boxes and bulletin boards, surveys (preferably conducted by individuals outside the library staff, in order to encourage honest reactions), informal observations made to library staff, and analyzing opinions expressed in the mass media. The use of mail-in coupons in newspapers has also been suggested.[14] These methods are far from satisfactory, and librarians, like others, keep open the search for new ways to find out more about their public image.

User surveys are a common feedback technique. One such study by a British library was conducted through a series of personal interviews, rather than the more common practice of distributing questionnaire forms in the library. Every fifth user of this library (a 20 per cent sample) was contacted, which involved 680 interviews. People leaving the library were interviewed in order to ascertain their level of satisfaction with the library visit just completed. The results of the survey disclosed that users found the building easy to find, to enter, and that it was open at the right times. (A cynic might suggest that for individuals who couldn't find the building, getting in, or the hours of opening wouldn't matter much.) The majority located the material they needed easily, although most did not consult staff members. When they did, staff was found to be

helpful most of the time. Slightly under half of those interviewed said they would like to know more about the library's
services. One of the most useful findings of the survey to the
library staff was the discovery that more users were interested
in periodicals than in other more traditional reference materials. The article acknowledged the need to reconsider the
collection in view of this finding, and the new opportunity to
better focus promotional material as a result of the survey. [15]

Surveys of the larger community and of potential users are
often called citizen surveys. Surveys of this sort may disclose
interesting, albeit somewhat dismaying, knowledge and attitudes about libraries. Citizen polls, most frequently conducted by public libraries, sometimes reveal that the majority
of the people in a community do not even know where the
library is located, or how it is funded, much less what the
services are. Most attitudes about the library, however, are
usually vaguely positive, even if little is known about the agency, including the fact that public libraries are generally local
government agencies and part of a usually suspect government
bureaucracy. Such vague concepts about libraries in the public sector have long presented a problem for library publicists.

Staff Feedback

Lack of feedback from staff is a problem for many library
administrators. Some of the obstacles to upward communication in organizations are

1/ Fear among employees that expressing their true feelings about the organization could be dangerous.
2/ Belief that disagreeing with the boss will result in no
promotions.
3/ Conviction that management is not really interested
in staff problems.
4/ Feeling that staff are not rewarded for good ideas.
5/ Lack of supervisory accessibility and responsiveness.
6/ Conviction that management doesn't react promptly
to problems. [16]

Feedback from staff is a particularly critical problem within organizations in connection with staff morale. Low morale may not be recognized by administrators. Such feedback is also an important source of information about library users and community citizens. If library employees don't pass on to the library administration what people are saying to them about the library, an important source of information for improving services and programs has been lost.

Planning Based on Evaluation

As stated earlier, it is essential to use the results of surveys and other forms of evaluation in planning for the library, not only in working on the library's image, but also in building its collections, services, and programs. Promotion should never be used to cover up or to rationalize problems. Here is one of the main differences between promotion per se and public relations/marketing. In public relations as a facet within the marketing structure, problems are identified and plans made to overcome them; they are not glossed over or used as justification for past inadequacies.

Continued PR/Marketing Development

Any process needs to be constantly refined and explored, and marketing is an area at present in which there is much fruitful investigation and potential for growth. Marketing research is seen as a primary activity in most commercial establishments today, because of its ability to identify buyer needs. This knowledge is valuable to the company in developing and designing products, packaging them appropriately, pricing them accurately and distributing them strategically in order to provide maximum exposure to potential buyers.

Public relations has not seen as much growth in recent decades as marketing, perhaps because its functions are quite clearly defined and these logically make it a part of the larger field of marketing. Some aspects of public relations are still ripe for development, however, primarily areas that are still weak, such as diagnostic and evaluation techniques.

By continuing to explore new approaches to marketing and public relations, librarians can keep these processes dynamic and growing, which is essential for keeping them relevant and up-to-date. If the processes become static, they tend to be treated as routine, and this can lead to disinterest and, finally, a poor job.

PR as a Year Round Activity

As a function within marketing, PR is sometimes seen as a tool for particular times, as in a company's crisis period. In a number of corporations the PR officers are used increasingly to train executives how to behave effectively before television cameras when disaster strikes. In times of crisis it is essential for the organization's spokesperson to behave calmly, rationally, exuding strength and purpose. Poor handling of a crisis situation may well result in adding to the company's already poor reputation, and contribute to its eventual downfall. The same principles apply to libraries.

But a public-relations officer is more than a speech coach. He/she is responsible for a company's year-round image projection, and makes use of the results of marketing research and planning. In the library that has not committed itself to planning, collections, services, and programs based solely on users' needs, the public relations staff person has a larger job, and must base image projection of the library on those philosophies of library service the administration has agreed to.

In any case, public relations is not a one-shot matter; the public relations office must maintain continuing contacts with a wide variety of people, including the mass media, influential community leaders, and community organizations. This is not only so that these contacts will be ready and can be called upon in times of trouble, but for their value as sources of feedback and help in initiating new services and programs.

Maintenance of existing service and program promotion is also important in public relations. Constant vigilance is needed throughout the year to focus attention on ongoing activities as well as the new.

Recognition of Benefits

Librarians are likely to use PR and marketing skillfully and to full advantage only when they have a clear understanding of the benefits to be derived from these functions. They should not be carried out as necessary evils, but rather as beneficial friends. With experienced and knowledgeable use comes recognition of their power. The good public relations officer and marketing vice-president are fully aware of what their respective functions are capable of achieving. For the less experienced in these fields there may be a tendency to be cautious or to hold back, and this can result in niggardly results and the self-justification of a reluctant administrator who is secretly proud of the conviction that PR and marketing "aren't what they're cracked up to be." A negative attitude usually breeds negative results.

Role of Participatory Management

In relation to both public relations and marketing participatory management is important in setting a library environment for their effective utilization. By involving the library staff in the management of the library—its planning, operations, and evaluation—the public relations and marketing functions will operate better, because everyone working for the goals and objectives of the library will contribute ideas for the various phases of both functions. Participatory management, by its very nature, is conducive to good communication and feedback, which in turn produce more information about the library's use and image. The more accurate the idea one has about the library's image, the better the plans that can be made for improved image projection.

References

1. Philip Lesly. "Emergency Principles and Trends," in *Lesly's Public Relations Handbook*, ed. by Philip Lesly. 2d ed. Englewood Cliffs, N.J., Prentice-Hall, 1978, pp. 601–14.

2. Benson Shapiro. "Marketing for Nonprofit Organizations," *Harvard Business Review* 51 (September–October 1973): 123.

3. Philip Kotler. *The Principles of Marketing*. Englewood Cliffs, N.J., Prentice-Hall, 1983, pp. 16–18.

4. *International Encyclopedia of the Social Sciences*, s.v. "Public Opinion," by Phillips Davison.

5. "Gallup Poll Finds a Rise in Belief in Newspapers," *New York Times*, July 29, 1979, p. F9.

6. Scott M. Cutlip and Allen H. Center. *Effective Public Relations*. 5th ed. Englewood Cliffs, N.J., Prentice-Hall, 1978, p. 66.

7. E. Bradford Burns. *A History of Brazil*. New York, Columbia University Press, 1970, p. 152.

8. Hadley Cantril. *Gauging Public Opinion*. Princeton, N.J., Princeton University Press, 1947, pp. 220–30.

9. David G. Myers. "How Groups Intensify Opinions," *Human Nature* (March 1979): 34–39.

10. Marvin Scilken. "Realism in Public Library Public Relations," *Library Journal* 97 (1 April 1972): 1246–47.

11. James G. Barnes and Ronald McTavish. "Segmenting Industrial Markets by Buyer Sophistication," *European Journal of Marketing* 17 (1983): 16–33.

12. Blaise Cronin. "The Marketing of Public Library Services in the United Kingdom—The Rationale for a Marketing Approach," *European Journal of Marketing* 18 (1984): 38.

13. Anne J. Matthews. "Library Market Segmentation: An Effective

Approach for Meeting Client Needs," *Journal of Library Administration* 5 (Fall 1984): 25–26.

14. Bob Usherwood. *The Visible Library: Practical Public Relations for Public Libraries.* London, The Library Association, 1981, p. 170.

15. A. Durcan. "A Reference Library Talks to Its Users," *European Journal of Marketing* 18 (1984): 65–71.

16. Albert Vogel. "Why Don't Employees Speak Up?" in *Communication in Organizations*, ed. by James L. Owen, Paul A. Page and Gordon I. Zimmerman. St. Paul, West, 1976, pp. 53–57.

IV PUBLIC RELATIONS: THE PROCESS AND PROGRAM PLANNING

As with any organizational function, a basic process exists for PR which describes the flow of that function. Many administrative processes exist within organizations, including libraries, such as budgetary control, personnel, and materials control. Public relations has its organizational processes also. They are logical ones, but variations can be created to meet the needs and objectives of the organization concerned. These processes also involve program planning. An examination of some typical public relations and marketing processes and program plans discloses similarities both in the overall functional flow and in certain components within the processes and the program plans.

Consideration of the process and program planning for PR and marketing helps to provide a basic understanding of how these functions work. By thinking through the actual steps that occur, it can be seen that public relations and marketing are appropriate functions within library organizations and that their intelligent use can be helpful in attaining the overall objectives of the library.

The Library Public Relations Process

Some contemporary PR specialists prefer to describe the public relations process as four simple sub-functions:

1/ Fact-finding
2/ Planning
3/ Communicating
4/ Evaluating[1]

This description is accurate enough, although a bit skeletal. Certainly, these four sub-functions are vital to the process. Fact-finding involves investigation of public attitudes and community analysis. Planning, in many ways the heart of the process, is the setting down of objectives, budget, timetable and tactics to be employed. Communication, probably the best-known and understood of these sub-functions, involves the various promotional activities and feedback systems set up by libraries to ensure two-way communication. Evaluating is perhaps the most elusive, since in a service, nonprofit organization measurement involves examination of results more complex than simple bottom-line statistics.

Another set of sub-functions for the PR process has been outlined by Philip Kotler:

1/ Identifying the organization's relevant publics.
2/ Measuring images and attitudes of the relevant publics toward the organization.
3/ Establishing image and attitude goals for the key publics.
4/ Developing cost-effective public relations strategies.
5/ Implementing actions and evaluating results.[2]

This process outline stresses the interrelationship between an organization and its publics, and demonstrates also the underlying importance of communication to public relations.

While the sub-functions of the PR process are of interest, it is with the development of the public relations program plan that the actual steps involved in carrying out the PR process can be more clearly seen. Examination of how the process works may provide a better understanding of its nature.

It might seem superfluous to justify the need for planning, but it should be stressed that planning has many benefits, including minimizing risk, reducing uncertainty, avoiding surprises, superimposing order and facilitating control.[3]

A *Library PR Program Plan*

Many program plans for public relations have been suggested through the years.[4] The one that follows incorporates the main features found in most planned library PR programs. Each of these steps is examined in depth following the general outline.

1/ Assess the current state of the library's PR, including the image projected and its perception, relationships with various audiences and overall status.

2/ Determine the strengths and weaknesses that currently exist in the libary's PR profile.

3/ Establish goals and objectives of the PR plan within the context of the overall library's mission, goals and objectives.

4/ Rank strengths and weaknesses in the current PR situation according to importance. (Determine which are problems needing to be resolved as soon as possible.) Make sure strengths and weaknesses are included in the PR goals and objectives.

5/ Establish a budget and a timetable and decide on techniques best suited to deal with problems. Provide a caretaking system to protect strengths.

6/ Determine evaluative techniques to measure degree of success in dealing with problems and maintaining or building on strengths.

7/ Communicate strategies to all staff of the library.

8/ Implement strategies.

9/ Encourage various feedbacks throughout the program.

10/ Evaluate the results of the program. Evaluate the effectiveness of the plan itself. Continue to plan (with or without modification) in order to keep an active PR in place.

Assess the Current PR of the Library

A number of important features are included in the overall assessment of a library's current public relations situation. The library planner must consider the various known publics of the library and their attitudes about the library, as well as the public as a whole. In the case of public libraries this means considering whole communities. In academic, school and special libraries, communities must be defined before considering their attitudes about the institution. Certain traditional publics have been associated through the years with various types of libraries. In the case of public libraries there are the traditional age groups, and special interest groups which have received attention at different times, such as business personnel, new immigrants, the blind and physically handicapped, and the disadvantaged. In academic and school libraries, there may be a variety of publics to be considered: not just faculty (teachers), administration, students, and governing bodies, but such peripheral groups as citizens in the community, parents, and segments of the larger scholarly community beyond the college and/or university. Special libraries often identify their publics in terms of their *raison d'être*; generally they comprise those individuals working within the corporation or government agency, plus a few, specified, specialized individuals.

Techniques for measuring attitudes about the library among the general public and its various segments include surveying, analysis of mass media coverage, and an honest appraisal of the library's status within the larger community. Other techniques have been devised by the commercial world, and have met with varying degrees of success.

Surveying has been used with some success for library self-assessment purposes. A number of types of surveys exist, some involving only library users, others covering the larger communities. The latter are often used to identify potential users.

The advantages and disadvantages of survey use have been much debated by librarians, but they continue to be used widely in spite of generally acknowledged flaws, including the skewing resulting from a polite public, the reluctance of respondents to take enough time to provide thoughtful responses, and the overall superficiality of results. Gathering information about public opinion is difficult for any institution, government, or business, but the use of surveys by means of questionnaires is still prevalent, in part because of the lack of any better technique for determining public attitudes. The greatest danger in libraries, and a regrettable current trend, is to see surveys as an end in themselves, rather than as an early step in the overall planning process.

Analysis of coverage in the mass media is another way to measure image. It also provides a clue to existing relationships with various audiences, since comments and reports on the library often not only reflect attitudes but indicate how the library gets along with the media and with various influential public groups.

Libraries traditionally keep scrapbooks of newspaper clippings about the library. These clippings can be categorized to answer a variety of questions or concerns. For example, did the library generate the press release used by the paper? Or did the library director suggest a feature story about the library to draw attention to National Library Week? Perhaps constructive coverage of library programs came as a surprise. Or negative letters to the editor by irate citizens may have prompted an exposé-type story. Citizens' groups are known to rally around the library in times of referendum drives. But they are also known to fight against new library buildings, because of financial stress. All these expressions in print reveal public attitudes. Librarians need to examine these newspaper items carefully, the negative as well as the positive, as partial barometers of public opinion.

The electronic media, particularly radio and television, may also cover library news and activities. It is, unfortunately, less easy to capture fleeting references from broadcasts, unless the library staff has been alerted in advance to the possibility of coverage. It is often necessary to rely on second-hand accounts of what was covered, making accurate assessment of the coverage more difficult. However, it is still possible at least to judge whether the coverage came about because of library generation or as a result of outside interest.

Another way to measure the library's reputation is to consider its status within the larger community. Ways to judge this are more elusive, but some are possible. For example, how do community leaders view appointment to the public library board? Is it as desirable and prestigious as an appointment to the board of the municipal zoo or the city human services boards? Do university professors tout the glories of their academic library, or do they talk about the necessity for improvement? Worse yet, do they not talk about it at all? Where is the special library placed on the organization chart of a corporation? Is it viewed by the administration as a vital link in the corporation's information flow, or is it relegated to uneasy status at a low level under a miscellaneous, catch-all department? All of these can be viewed as symptomatic indicators of the library's status.

Establish Goals and Objectives for a PR Program

The beginning of a plan for a library's PR program is an examination of the library's basic mission, and of its goals and objectives. Most statements of goals and objectives will include items that relate directly or indirectly to the library's public relations, such as increased book circulation, heightened awareness of the library's services by certain audiences, and improved financial support. These goals and objectives should be incorporated into the individualized PR program goals and objectives. In addition, those who are formulating the PR program plan will no doubt include other goals and objectives, some perhaps relating to particular departments within the library and some distinct to the PR function itself. For example, a department objective might be increasing use of a parents' shelf in the children's room. A related PR objective that might well be decided upon (in cooperation with the children's room staff) is identifying means for helping achieve this objective through precise definition of target audiences and the development of communication techniques to reach those audiences. This latter type of objective, distinct to the PR process itself, might include such items as increased coverage of library activities in the local media.

In the formation of goals and objectives for a library's PR program, just as with those for the institution, two factors need to be kept in mind: 1/ objectives should be phrased in measurable terms, and 2/ constant revision of the goals and objectives is necessary to keep the program current and vital.

Stating objectives in measurable terms makes the job of evaluation much easier. It provides a clear statement of the desired outcome of certain activities and helps the planner set realistic outcomes within reasonable time-frames. In public relations attention to details is important, as is the achievement of seemingly small objectives that combine and culminate in the improved overall image of the library.

If the planner concentrates on smaller objectives, it is likely that these objectives will need constant revision. Since objectives are generally parts of larger, possibly unattainable goals, it may not be necessary to rephrase the goals as often. Nevertheless, goals, as well as objectives, need to be reviewed periodically and perhaps more frequent editing will be required for the more sweeping, general, idealized goals. In particular, it is important for the PR planner to keep the PR goals and objectives current with those of the library as a whole and its various departments.

Examples of library public relations goals and objectives can be found in the basic documents of many libraries. A typical PR goal might be: increasing public awareness about the library and its services. An objective under such a goal could be the submission of a weekly library column to a local newspaper for publication.

Review and revision of a library's PR program goals is the area of the plan most often neglected. Once the difficult, time-consuming, and sometimes tedious task of setting goals and objectives is completed the first time around, there is often a tendency to think of them as permanent. Or the planner and implementer find it more fun to work with tactics, thus relegating the goals and objectives, once set, to a less vital part of the program continuum. Over the long haul this can result in confusion, since the PR implementer cannot act without reference to the library as a whole. The library's PR goals and objectives must be constantly kept in line with the overall directions of the organization. New and/or increased services should be coordinated with public relations planning in order to give them every opportunity for success.

Determine Strengths and Weaknesses

The determination of strengths and weaknesses in the existing PR program is a hard, soul-searching step in the overall planning process. We tend to point with pride to our successes, but do not like to remember our failures. There is also a reluctance to consider that some successes may be temporary and contain elements which may lead to failure in the long run. For example, increased circulation is generally seen as a success, but if budgets are not increased to maintain the book stock at an adequate level, the increased circulation can lead ultimately to a higher rate of user frustration. It would be a mistake, though, to go to extremes and become too cautious, viewing all strengths, like a prophet of doom, as potential problems.

After information about the library's image, relationships and status has been collected, it should be sifted in order to separate the good from the bad. At this point it is probably better to be overly critical and not look for silver linings. Not everything that appears bad on the surface is necessarily terrible, but it is worth keeping in mind the superficial manner in which many library communication messages are received. Many individual library users do not always think through the complexities of mixed messages and their seemingly negative aspects. Chicagoans are more likely to remember the large front-page headline in a Sunday newspaper proclaiming "Library in Chaos" than favorable comments appearing in letters to the editor.

It is too simplistic to call a bad press merely "a PR problem." By analyzing and pinpointing shortcomings, tactics can be developed to deal with criticism. In determining strengths in the PR image of the library, one needs to consider whether the library capitalizes on these strengths. For example, is the main building considered a source of pride by many in the community? If so, is it included on tours?

It is not always easy to decide upon strengths or weaknesses. There may be, for example, a lack of public outcry over a cutback in hours of service. Some library personnel may breathe a sigh of relief and consider this a result of public understanding, but it may be more symptomatic of public apathy. At first glance a school librarian might consider a modest number of requests from teachers for items from a booklist to be a success, but a glance in the trashbins behind the school might reveal the majority of lists discarded if an unsolicited distribution has been made to all teachers.

Assessment of the library's reputation and the determination of its strengths and weaknesses are sometimes painful for the librarian. It is, apparently, a professional weakness to want to think that others believe in libraries as strongly as librarians do. It is hard to take criticism well and use it to good purpose. It is also hard to accept the fact that the PR operation is a constant struggle; it is not a job that is ever completed. Its very continuing nature makes it a process that must be constantly watched and improved upon.

Once strengths and weaknesses have been determined, they should be ranked in order of importance. In other words, rank them by degree of "goodness" and "badness." Consider not only the PR activity that is being ranked, but also any library operation related to it. For example, a surprise appearance by the local mini-cam crew of a local television news service to cover a disastrous flood in the basement stacks could be viewed as playing up a problem, or giving a negative impression, but the result could well be to bring public attention to bear on the problem in a positive, helpful way.

Flat-out failures are probably the hardest to deal with honestly. We tend to rationalize failures, rather than examine them objectively. If a program or service gets little or no response, one should look at that failure carefully as a learning experience. Librarians should consider what the original intent of the program was, why a particular course of action was selected, what was done, what the results of that action were, and finally, why expectations were not met.[5] Never dismiss failure with a simple explanation such as, "It was a bad night; too many other things going on." We need to see whether the basic program idea and format were at fault.

The final part of this process is to decide which problems (weaknesses) need to be dealt with immediately, and which can be considered later. A separate timetable can be set to deal with the problems alone, but one should also keep working on the strengths so that the successes do not slip away.

Budget, Timetable and Tactics

If a careful assessment of PR problems and strengths has been made, all fronts should be covered, with no pockets of neglect. By emphasizing problem areas first, library PR planners may head off potential disasters, thus avoiding the PR specialist's greatest dread, crisis PR. Crisis public relations is dreaded mostly because of the lasting damage that can be caused to an organization's image. A negative image, such as that arising from embezzlement of funds from the library's coffers, is hard to dispel. An episode of this kind is likely to be remembered by the public much longer than more positive PR images.

Selecting tactics and techniques falls into that area of public relations which has generally received the most attention: promotion and publicity. Since these activities are dealt with later (see Chapter 7), lengthy discussion is not necessary here. It should be noted, though, that this stage of the program plan is when those techniques are selected which seem to have most potential for creating positive images. A decision might be made, for example, to use a mass-media campaign rather than purely in-house promotion of a worthy service that is not being sufficiently used. Conversely, it might be decided that individuals who are already library users should be the target group for promotion of a new service. Whatever the decision, it is often made within the context of time and cost. These two factors are not necessarily constrictive controls, although they are too often used as such in library settings.

Another important element in the determination of techniques, time, and budget is the staff needed to carry out the plan once it has been formulated. This, also, can be a restrictive feature in library PR planning, for in lean economic times libraries tend to have few individuals who can be spared for special efforts beyond their primary job responsibilities.

Evaluation Techniques

There are a variety of methods of evaluation and they have been used with varying degrees of success (see Chapter 8). It is important, however, to select the most appropriate method of evaluation for each public-relations activity. Counting inches of newspaper space is not a particularly appropriate way to measure the success of a new service. The best technique is to examine the use of and reaction to the new service, not the amount of publicity it has received. This aspect of the public relations plan underscores the inseparability of public relations from the rest of library operations. It is possible to discuss the function as a separate process, but it cannot be evaluated separately. Its basic purpose is too closely allied to the purpose of the entire library.

It is worth repeating that the evaluation techniques decided upon must include measurement of those public relations areas which were previously judged as satisfactory and successful. By constant evaluation it is possible to safeguard against possible slippage in the positive public relations area. Also, the time and cost of evaluation must be included as part of the overall budget for any public relations program.

Staff Communication

Vital to any public relations program is the knowledgeable involvement of the library staff in its execution. Whenever possible, library staff should be included in all phases of PR program planning, but it is essential that all staff be made aware of ongoing and future PR activities. The best plans can be easily undermined by uninformed staff members who are not committed to the library's goals and objectives.

In addition to knowing what is going on and why, the staff needs to be aware of how it will happen. The strategies, timing, and possible problems need to be explained, so that staff members will be able to respond to questions from the public. It is critical that staff be informed before strategies are implemented, although this may present problems. For example, it may be necessary for a board to take action before a new service can be announced, and the press may get hold of the information before the staff. If the staff is unaware of the action until it has hit the newspapers and the public has begun to demand the service, staff members, reasonably enough, may be irritated over not being forewarned, particularly if a policy change is involved. It is far better to alert the staff that the board action may take place, giving them some opportunity to prepare for the impact of the proposed change.

Implementation

In many ways one of the most difficult aspects of planning is the actual implementation of a program. It is easy to be seduced by the charms of playing the "what if" game during earlier stages of planning, and far more difficult to put the plan into action and see whether it will work or not.

It is therefore important to include an implementation date in the plan's timetable and stick to it as closely as possible. Although it is wise to plan carefully, there comes a time when one must act if a new program or service is ever to take effect. One reason why it is hard to implement plans is the uncertainty of knowing whether they will be successful at the point of implementation, the moment when the solid force of reality comes in confrontation with dreams.

Feedback

Feedback needs to be soliciated at every stage of a new plan's implementation. Some aspect of the program can easily be overlooked, but it can be corrected without serious impact if caught quickly enough. As an example, scheduling a new series of programs for the same weeknight that had been devoted to meetings of a community group would alienate the very audience the series was designed to attract. It is better for the library to change the program night than to declare the programs a failure. Be adaptable whenever possible.

Feedback can be solicited in a variety of ways. Talk to people using the new service or coming to the new program. Find out what appealed to them about the new offering. If you expected a better response, ask the users why they think it's not more popular. If the library has a suggestion box or a bulletin board for patrons, check it carefully during early days of implementation to see whether there are criticisms of the new service or program. There can be perils in feedback, as with any activity, as Will Manley noted after a series of negative comments appeared on a suggestion board in his library:

> After several moments of silence, one of the children's librarians bravely asked, "Why did you put the comment board up in the first place? You said you wanted to hear from the public."
> "Yes," I answered, "I guess I thought they were going to tell us how great we are."[6]

Another method for encouraging feedback is to ask librarians who are giving public presentations to include information about the new service or program and have them gauge (subjectively, to be sure) whether there appears to be interest when the group is told about the new offering. Also, keep a keen eye out for any notices of the new service or program in newspapers and other local mass media. Most such notices, of course, will be generated by the library itself, but occasionally a radio disc jockey will add personal comments, such as, "Sounds good to me," or a newspaper may be prompted to do an editorial.

The final, important feedback is use. Whether or not, and how, individuals use the new service or program is the most crucial test of all.

Evaluation

The feedback reactions and certainly the actual use made of the program are important in evaluation. An output measure such as use may not, however, be the only criterion used in evaluation, for some new services and programs may not be intended for a large number of people. In such cases a more subjective evaluation may need to be made as well, such as estimating the degree of gratitude of those who do use the offering.

In most cases, though, it is use which determines the degree of success of a new program or service. In our society cost-effectiveness is what seems to count most. It is a quantitative way to measure performance, but quantitative measures are often inadequate or hard to determine for evaluating good will or an improved public image, two of the most basic reasons to have a public relations program.

References

1. ALA *World Encyclopedia of Library and Information Science*, s.v., "Public Relations," by Peggy Barber.

2. Philip Kotler. *Marketing for Nonprofit Organizations*. 2d ed. Englewood Cliffs, N.J., Prentice-Hall, 1982, p. 382.

3. Dorothy J. Anderson. "The High Cost of Planning," *Journal of Library Administration* 6 (Spring 1965): 10.

4. An early plan presented by Edward Bernays in his book *Public*

Relations (Norman, Okla., University of Oklahoma Press, 1951, pp. 9–10) includes the following:

1/ Definition of objectives
2/ Definition of public to be reached
3/ Modification of objectives in light of the public, so that *attainable* goals are set
4/ Strategy
5/ Tactics and timing
6/ Culmination of tactics and evaluation of each phase of the program.

5. Cosette Kies. *Projecting a Positive Image Through Public Relations.* Chicago, American Association of School Librarians/American Library Association, 1979, pp. 21–22.

7. Will Manley. "Facing the Public," *Wilson Library Bulletin* 59 (February 1985): 399.

V MARKETING: THE PROCESS AND SYSTEM

In the marketing process, more emphasis is laid on a variety of precise analytical techniques than holds for public relations in the narrow sense. Also, marketing in practice is a system, laid out carefully according to certain principles. Some purposes of this process may not always directly relate to libraries, such as the importance of identifying new markets and of diversification. These concepts may be appropriate for some libraries, depending on their mission statements, goals, and objectives, but they should be applied only where appropriate.

Philip Kotler proposes the following outline for a marketing management process:

1/ Analyzing market opportunities
    1.1/ Marketing research and information systems
    1.2/ The marketing environment
    1.3/ Consumer markets
    1.4/ Organizational markets
2/ Selecting target markets
    2.1/ Measuring and forecasting demand
    2.2/ Market segmentation, targeting, and positioning
3/ Developing the marketing mix
    3.1/ Designing products
    3.2/ Pricing products
    3.3/ Placing products
    3.4/ Promoting products
4/ Managing the marketing effort
    4.1/ Strategic planning and marketing planning
    4.2/ Marketing organization and control.[1]

Rephrased for nonprofit organizations such as libraries, this process could be described as comprising four steps: 1/ analyzing the community; 2/ identifying, segmenting, and selecting target groups; 3/ designing and promoting appropriate programs for these groups; and 4/ managing the process through planning, research and control. On further examination it can be seen that no part of this process is new to libraries.

Community Analysis

Finding ways to know more about the community the library is intended to serve has been a time-honored practice in librarianship, although most prevalent in public libraries. Today the stress placed on community analysis by public librarians is very evident. Other types of libraries—academic, school and special—have begun to pay more attention to this aspect of marketing recently. If nothing else, they recognize the need to identify primary groups of users and other potential users.

Academic and school librarians have long practiced segmentation, identifying such major groups within their communities as students, faculty/teachers, administration, and staff. The importance of such other groups as citizens of the town in which the academic and/or school library is located, and individuals and groups responsible for funding, depends on the philosophy of the individual institution. Special librarians, also, have often taken the time to identify groups of users and nonusers, examining wider communities in order to identify them. Such analysis is helpful not only in planning for marketing and public relations, but vital in policy development.

Target Groups

In libraries there has been a tendency to identify and label our user and potential user groups in fairly easy, concrete demographic terms. Another obvious method of identification is based on geographic distinctions, such as taxpayers within certain boundaries, or individuals residing in a certain county. In marketing circles, however, other variables include psychographic and behavioral segmentation.

Psychographic segmentation is a system of dividing groups on the basis of life style, social class and, sometimes, personality. For example, much current commercial marketing interest is focused on "yuppies," generally characterized as fairly affluent, upwardly mobile, urban professionals with certain likes and dislikes. A parallel for such a grouping in librarianship could be readers, defined as individuals who regularly read books for pleasure and self-education.

A categorization developed in the 1970s, the Vals Framework developed by Arnold Mitchell, was based on analysis of extensive questionnaires directed to nearly 3,000 individuals. These categories are arranged in certain basic development stages, such as the need-driven stage. The nine categories are

1/ Survivors: disadvantaged individuals who are often depressed and withdrawn.
2/ Sustainers: disadvantaged individuals who are trying to escape from the poverty trap.
3/ Belongers: conventional people who would rather be part of a group than experiment on their own.
4/ Emulators: ambitious individuals, such as yuppies.
5/ Achievers: leaders, those who have it made and enjoy life as it is.
6/ "I-am-me": self-engrossed people, often teenagers.
7 Experientials: happy individuals who want to experience what life has to offer.
8/ Societally conscious: individuals with social responsibility who want to make the world a better place.
9/ Integrateds: fully psychologically matured individuals who are well adjusted to themselves and the world.[2]

A categorization of this kind can be very useful in commercial marketing, although its use in library marketing would seem to be limited. Little examination of this sort has been done, however, outside of a few articles, such as one by Michael Madden in which certain characteristics of groups of readers and nonreaders are described.[3] The library field lacks a psychology and sociology of readers and readership.

One life-style study by Theodore Bolton concludes that as library usage increases, individuals tend to: have more self-confidence, be more optimistic about the future, enjoy travel and be more interested in foreign countries, have a more contemporary outlook on life, be more financially secure, be more diet-conscious, read about and listen to fewer sporting events and enjoy television less.[4] Interpretations of such relationships waits upon more data.

Appeals based on class and lifestyle, not to mention aspiration to be part of certain class groups, have been used for years. One early example is a broadside urging support of the public library acts in Bath, England. This poster asked, "Working-Men, have you compared the Men who ask you to Vote for the Half-penny Rate with those who say don't?" Following are two columns for the "Yes" and "No" voters. "Yes" voters include: the Mayor and all the Corporation, the Whole of the Clergy of all Denominations, and all those who usually start and support plans intended to help the WORKING CLASSES. The "No" column, on the other hand, lists: "Mr. Osmond, of the Cremorne Tavern, Mr. Leader of the Angel Inn, Mr. Wartenburg, Beerseller, Captain Fitzgerald of the 'Angus,' and Mr. Reuben Cook, Commercial Traveller."[5]

Social class is a distinction generally avoided by Americans, probably because of the democratic belief in equality. Social classes there are, however, sometimes identified in ways other than the traditional upper, middle, and lower classes (with gradations in between, such as upper middle) by terms such as "blue collar" and "nouveau riche." Although librarians have liked to believe that readers and library users come from all classes, such early studies as one by William Converse Haygood[6] showed that public libraries were not used by a cross section of the American public, but rather by a preponderance of certain types, such as high school and college students. Bernard Berelson in his landmark analysis of 1949 identified the typical public library user as white, middle-class, educated, and female.[7] The most recent national study of library use, done by Gallup in 1978, showed typical users to be 18–34 years of age, college-educated, living in a household with children under 18, and residents of the Eastern part of the United States.[8]

Personality is the least applicable of the psychographic elements to library use. In commercial marketing, personality is used to key and identify certain brand products with certain desirable personality traits: masculine, luxurious, dependable, sophisticated, and the like, in order to attract these personality types to particular products. One of the best illustrations of this kind of marketing is the case of Marlboro cigarettes, which had originally been viewed as a "weaker" tobacco and hence a "feminine" product. In an effort to turn this image around, the company marketers launched a campaign using the Marlboro man, a tough, macho westerner with a tattoo on his hand.

Behavioral segmentation is based in the world of commerce on the degree of product and brand loyalty exhibited by individuals. Groupings can be described as very loyal, casual switchers, or indifferent consumers. Brand loyalty is obviously the desired result of much marketing. Buyer behavior that will result in purchase even if other brands are a better buy is the aim. This, also, has little application to library operations.

Product loyalty, on the other hand, does seem to have some relationship to libraries. Product loyalty is the motivation to use or obtain something which is often not a necessity. Such items might be fresh-cut flowers for one's own home, or a snowmobile for winter sport. Some people view the library's "products"—books, records, videotapes and other library materials—as luxury items. In the case of the library, product loyalty means motivating individuals to want to come to your "shop" and "buy" your goods. In simple terms, people considered to be loyal to our products are those who are good library users.

The design and promotion of appropriate library programs for segments identified as being useful groups for cultivation is where much marketing effort is concentrated. In the commercial world, the marketing mix has been regarded over the past few decades as the key to success or failure. In librarianship we do not think of ourselves as being much involved in designing products and pricing and placing them, but we have long recognized the need to promote our "products": library materials, services and special programs.

The Marketing Mix

Librarians do, however, need to concern themselves with design, price, and placement, because they are already involved with these matters. The marketing mix, consisting of product design, packaging, pricing, placement, and promotion, has definite library application.

Librarians are responsible for product design of basic book collections, as well as of special collections. A decision to establish a collection of children's toys and games (realia) is a design decision in the sense that librarians thereby provide a new service. Certainly, librarians design programs, as well, programs they hope will attract people to the library.

In the matter of packaging there is one area which is easy to overlook; the packages library materials come in when purchased—book jackets, record sleeves, and the like. These items are often designed (packaged) to help sales in stores, and great deliberation goes into what color to make a book jacket, the evolution of genre paperback covers, the use of embossing, cut-outs, and other graphic attractions to entice browsers to buy.[9] Publishers generally do not share the results of their marketing experimentation with book jacket design, but successful formulas can obviously be detected if one studies the bookstore shelves over a period of time. Certain designs must be successful, or they wouldn't be used repeatedly by the same publisher and imitated by others.

Research on what library users think of book covers has been very limited. One study, done in 1982 by Laura-Ellen Ayers, focussed on the cover designs of six teen-age "problem" novels and questioned 25 young women in a private prep school. Forty per cent of the students selected the same title to read when asked their preference. The reason given most often for the choice was vague, such as "Looks good," but some said they liked the idea of the main characters being their own age.[10] The value of such surveys is that they help us understand why people select the titles they do when browsing for something to read. Librarians have probably underestimated the importance of cover art in guiding an individual to make that first move to pick up a book and consider it for possible reading. Only recently have many libraries started to look at merchandising techniques in displaying books and other library materials effectively.

Another type of packaged material commonly found in libraries is magazines. Covers of popular magazines are generally designed to attract customers at the point of purchase, rather than through subscription alone. It has been demonstrated repeatedly that one thing on which magazines sell more copies than any other subject is sex. This can be demonstrated by the variation in monthly sales for *Sports Illustrated*. It generally sells around 250,000 copies per issue, but the annual swimsuit issue of 1984, featuring a scantily clad female model, sold over twice that number.[11]

There are other examples of packaging which can be applied in libraries. Titles are an important part of a movie's packaging,[12] and the movie's name can be used for promotion in library publicity. Another area in which a library can use packaging is in the graphic image (appearance of printed materials) and the signs used throughout the library. Some attention has been given recently to the importance of signage in libraries,[13] and it should be considered not just as a tool to assist library users in finding their way in the building, but in its aesthetic sense of projecting a strong, professional image of an organization that cares about its appearance.

The matter of pricing has been faced already in most libraries in connection, for example, with coin-operated copying machines and pay telephones. Among other long-term accepted fee services is interlibrary loan. With the advent of online searches the "free versus fee" debate has become heated over whether the ranks of information poor will be enlarged if charges are made for online services. As long as material obtained via an online search is also available through the longer, more tedious hand-search process (free), one can perhaps justify charging for more expensive online searches. But the question remains: if material is available *only* through electronic data bases, should many people be deprived of information because they cannot afford fees set by the library? The arrival on the scene of commerical and independent information brokers has added to the confusion, for they must charge fees in order to stay in business, and they are in competition, in some cases, with libraries which may provide similar searches at less cost, or no cost at all.

Traditionally, libraries, when charging for services such as telephone calls or copies on a reproduction machine have charged only enough to cover costs (and sometimes only a portion of that), or perhaps enough more to make a slight profit to help with library expenses. It is, of course, difficult to price, for this involves balancing what it costs to provide an item against what is felt to be "fair." It is difficult even to establish the true cost of a service, for if overhead charges, including a proportion of the cost of providing the library building, staff, etc., are built into the cost, the end price may be much too high for many individuals to pay. [14]

Another aspect of pricing is the ownership of data bases, bringing up the question of what information should be free for all. Beyond the cost of tapping into various data bases is the fact that some are private and cannot be used at all by outside sources, another limitation on free access to information for all. [15]

Placement in libraries involves the locations of service points, as well as of displays and location of materials and services within individual library buildings. It is concerned also with the relative ease and quickness of obtaining inter-library-loan materials. This is very similar to the role of placement in commercial marketing, which concentrates on outlets to carry products, and the placement of those products in the stores.

Darlene Weingand suggests that placement is an area with which libraries need to be more concerned, since distribution lends itself to analysis based on location, availability (hours open) and use statistics. One of her suggestions is to utilize a cable network channel to provide information during those hours when no library building is open.[16]

The final "P" of the marketing mix is promotion, an aspect of public relations and marketing covered at length in Chapter 7.

Positioning

Placement can be seen to have some relationship to positioning, a fairly new and interesting concept in marketing. Positioning means not physical placement of the product, but the place of a product in the potential buyer's mind. What and where are primary considerations involved in positioning. For example, most individuals have favorite cola drinks they buy; hence the "Pepsi Challenge," a campaign aimed to reposition Pepsi over Coke as the preferred brand to purchase.[17]

Positioning can also relate to the image of itself the organization intends to project. A library may decide to change its basic focus from that of a traditional book-oriented institution to a multimedia collection with attendant programs and services. Such a repositioning is a major step, and will require a whole new concept of marketing, one based on the "new" library's image.[18]

Positioning and repositioning are often thought of in terms of product brand names, and the desire to create brand loyalty. In libraries, however, one can see a relationship with location, or place. In this scenario the steps made by individuals who seek books should be traced. If the books wanted are desired for permanent ownership, then the library has lost in the first round. In some cases, though, there are additional considerations, such as cost (will the potential buyer want to buy an expensive book?), and time (will the potential buyer be willing to wait while a bookstore orders a book not in stock?). With a bookstore as the place of first position, readers have a better chance of immediately obtaining a bestseller, which they then also own. With the library as a place of first position, readers have a wider selection (usually) than a bookstore, and the option of interlibrary loan or reserve if the book is not in or not owned by the library. Individual choices of this kind determine where the reader goes to get a desired book, and the library may not be in first position.

Libraries have a more difficult job in positioning than many commercial establishments. Will Manley has contrasted libraries with McDonald's in terms of positioning. One reason for the fast-food franchise's great success is specialization in certain items, with little attempt to individualize. Libraries, on the other hand, try to serve the countless information needs of many individuals. As a result, libraries' degree of success cannot compare with that of an institution that specializes.[19]

Special libraries are generally better equipped to position collections and services to meet patron needs. Because they are usually established to serve a specialized clientele for a special purpose, their basic goals are clearer. It has been argued, however, that special librarians have to be careful to keep the library's goals and objectives aligned with those of the parent company, repositioning the library's collections and services as necessary to maintain as good a match as possible with the company's purposes.[20]

Product Life Cycle

Commercial companies are greatly concerned with product life cycles. Every product goes from a stage when it is new, through a period of growth when it is subject to peer acceptance, then into maturation, and finally perhaps into decline. Companies, clearly, want to keep products in the mature stage as long as possible, but they are also aware of the need to develop new products, so that they will always have goods in various stages of the product life cycle.

If we look at some current products, we can easily see what stage of the product life cycle they are in at present. VCRs for the home are probably still in the developing stage. Peer pressure may not yet have influenced the choice of a particular brand by members of a group; the main decision is whether or not to buy at all. Home computers, on the other hand, have been on the market for a longer time and the focus now appears to be on which brand, which make, to purchase. Peer pressure is a factor in this stage of maturity. In the declining stages, as in the case of home video games, the game itself is more important than the name of the company producing the game.

Libraries, too, have "products" which have life cycles. Some services go through cycles of popularity; others remain apparently strong for long periods of time. Some parts of the book collection go through life cycles, as do library programs on certain subjects. Some services, such as children's story hours, never seem to go out of fashion or decline in popularity, but certain program topics, such as current events or international politics, do not enjoy the popularity that they once did. Ideally, a library should have a range of services evenly spaced through different stages of the life cycle, so that the library is not totally dependent on the loyalty of those patrons who cling to traditional services in the waning stages of their life cycle.[21]

It has been suggested that products are failures only if they do not live up to expectations. Others have claimed one reason why products fail is because of the lack of proper marketing analysis. In the library's book collection in the light of such assertions, it should be remembered that the collection has been selected over a long period of time, under different collection philosophies, and possibly for different long-term purposes. When many public libraries were founded it was accepted by most libraries that selecting what people ought to read was more important than buying what they wanted to read. This has changed today in many libraries, although the desire to keep collections balanced and to purchase quality whenever possible remains strong. If there are varied reasons why librarians buy books, should the collection be deemed a failure if all the books in it do not circulate at similar levels? There is the kind of complexity which sometimes defies efforts to apply neat marketing theory to library situations.

It is possible, nevertheless, to apply marketing theory more accurately to some library programs and services. For example, if few people come to a highly touted brown-bag luncheon with a guest speaker, then it may be that the intended audience has no interest, and the program should probably be classified as a failure and analyzed in that light. On the other hand, some variations in format and speakers may determine that the basic idea was fine, but that something else may have caused the first program to fail, such factors as poor weather, unpopularity of the speaker, or disinterest in the subject.

Managing the Marketing Process

Finally, the management of the marketing process is little different in the profit and nonprofit worlds. Although the ultimate mission of the organizations may be different, the actual process and its management are not nearly so. As in any other operation, planning is essential for reasoned and effective efforts. Research is particularly vital in marketing and is probably the one characteristic which has provided marketing with its dynamism. In commerce, much time and money are spent in this area and research is often viewed as the essential key to a company's ultimate success or failure.

Control of the entire process must be centered at the management level, because of its crucial role in the institution's progress. Without top-level control, marketing becomes splintered, diversified, unfocused. Great care is needed to project strong, clear images of the institution to the various potential markets, and without the cohesion supplied by centralized management a single, unified image of the institution and its services is rarely likely to be achieved.

References

1. Philip Kotler. *Principles of Marketing*. 2d ed. Englewood Cliffs, N.J., Prentice-Hall, 1983, p. 33.

2. Arnold Mitchell. *The Nine American Life Styles*. New York, Macmillan, 1983.

3. Michael Madden. "Marketing Survey Spinoff: Library User/Nonuser Lifestyles," *American Libraries* 10 (February 1974): 78–81.

4. W. Theodore Bolton. "Life Style Research," *Library Journal* 107 (15 May 1982): 965–66.

5. Thomas Kelly. *Books for the People: An Illustrated History of the British Public Library.* London, Andre Deutsch, 1977, p. 84.

6. William Converse Haygood. *Who Uses the Public Library?* Chicago, University of Chicago Press, 1936.

7. Bernard Berelson. *The Library's Public: A Report of the Public Library Inquiry.* New York, Columbia University Press, 1949.

8. *A Perspective on Libraries: Facts, Figures and Opinions About Libraries and Reading.* Chicago, American Library Association, 1978, p. 7.

9. Cosette Kies. "The Packaging We Love So Much," *International Journal of Instructional Media,* 3 (1975–76): 261–68.

10. Laura-Ellen Ayers. "Cover Illustration in Young Adult Literature." Unpublished paper. Nashville, Department of Library and Information Science, Peabody College, Vanderbilt University, 1982.

11. Michael Gross. "Sex Sells," *Saturday Review* (July/August 1985): 50.

12. Candice Russell. "What's in a Film Name? It May Hold the Title to a Movie's Success," *Chicago Tribune,* June 2, 1985, Section 13, pp. 26–27.

13. For example: Dorothy Pollett and Peter C. Haskell, eds. *Sign Systems for Libraries.* New York, Bowker, 1979. And: H. Spencer and Linda Reynolds. *Directional Signing and Labelling in Libraries and Museums: A Review of Current Theory and Practice.* London, British Libraries' Research and Development Report 5415, 1977.

14. Andrea C. Dragon. "Librarians and Pricing," *Public Library Quarterly* 5 (Summer 1984): 23–25.

15. Leigh Estabrook. "Productivity, Profit, and Libraries," *Library Journal* 106 (July 1981): 1377–80.

16. Darlene E. Weingand. "Distribution of the Library's Product: The Need for Innovation," *Journal of Library Administration* 5 (Fall 1984): 49–57.

17. Al Ries and Jack Trout. *Positioning: The Battle for Your Mind.* New York, Warner, 1981.

18. Andrea C. Dragon and Tony Leisner. "The ABCs of Implementing Library Marketing," *The Journal of Library Administration* 5 (Fall 1984): 37–38.

19. Will Manley. "Facing the Public," *Wilson Library Bulletin* 55 (June 1981): 762–63, 98.

20. Arthur Sterngold. "Marketing for Special Libraries and Information Centers: The Positioning Process," *Special Libraries* 73 (October 1982): 254–259.

21. Pat Colman. "Public Libraries Can and Do Make a Difference: A Case to be Proved," *European Journal of Marketing* 18 (1984): 57.

VI THE PRACTICE OF LIBRARY MARKETING AND PUBLIC RELATIONS

IT IS POSSIBLE to gain some feeling for how librarians feel about public relations and marketing by examining the library literature, but that is only one reflection of how they actually practice it. A look at the practice of PR/marketing in libraries shows why libraries have had some problems in projecting a strong, positive image through the years.

A quick glance at comments about public relations and marketing in the past few decades shows a continuing variety of attitudes toward these processes. Some library administrators, such as Fred Glazer, State Librarian of West Virginia, strongly support the use of promotion techniques:

> Hard selling of libraries to the public is necessary if we are to create a significant demand for services. Once an awareness of libraries is established to a far greater degree than is now apparent, an agitated citizenry becomes the muscle used to wedge open the door for expanded library service. [1]

In Glazer's case his actions have supported his words, and his activities in West Virginia have served to substantially increase library budgets and public support for libraries. Others have urged increased use of library PR and marketing to improve support of libraries, though few have produced results as dramatic as those in West Virginia.

Some cautions and thoughtful concerns have been expressed as well, as in this comment by Arthur Curley, now Director of the Boston Public Library:

> Just query your friendly neighborhood random sample and see what feedback you get on libraries and librarians. Ironically, the responses may seem positive at first glance. Within the framework of conditioned expectations, we rate fairly well. But it is damning praise, for those expectations are pathetically low. The irate patron is something of a rarity, and actually a compliment to us, since his frustration is a function of high expectations. Most library users don't expect much, so they are easily pleased and merely shrug shoulders when disappointed. Of course, most people don't use libraries at all, but have nothing against them since they offer no serious threat to pride or purse. [2]

In addition to Curley's warning about public apathy, library literature features some cautions about PR and marketing. John Berry, editor of *Library Journal*, suggests that librarians need to take a hard, self-appraising look at their libraries and determine how accurate the image is that enthusiastic librarians try to project to the public. If libraries and librarians cannot and do not come through with the services and materials they promise, he says, no public relations and marketing efforts are better than those that mislead. [3] His points are well taken. Librarians are, of course, strongly biased in favor of libraries, and sometimes their enthusiasms are projected to show the agency as what they would like, and not in terms of the reality.

As responsible communicators librarians must deliver the things promised about the library, or they may find themselves in the position of the heroine of an old Frank Capra movie, of whom a character says, "Mary? She never married. She's just about to close up the library."[4] We may have to close up our libraries for good.

Some changes have occurred since the earlier days of library literature as reviewed in chapter one. There are few individuals now who actively scorn public relations and promotion activities, but one can find more subtle arguments for not employing them to full advantage. There would appear to be a growing consciousness among librarians as to what public relations is and what it is capable of doing. There are still those librarians who like to think that good libraries speak for themselves, but they are fewer in numbers. A particularly interesting change in PR attitudes has come about in academic libraries, where the need for fund-raising and friends groups has become more widely recognized. In the words of O. D. Hardison, Jr., then Director of the Folger Shakespeare Library:

> The fact that the operating funds of research libraries come from society or special interest groups in society creates what might be called the imperative of responsiveness. It is an imperative that has always been understood by public libraries, but one that until recently has been less apparent to research libraries. The reason for it, of course, is money. [5]

While in both larger public and academic libraries there has been, apparently, a growing acceptance of public relations, it is still difficult to determine attitudes and practice regarding marketing activities. Few libraries have made the full commitment that the Denver Public Library has to a marketing philosophy and the hiring of a marketing director for the agency. In this chapter we deal primarily with the practice of library public relations, and although many smaller libraries have practiced PR successfully, attention will be focused on the larger libraries which have separated PR as an identifiable activity. In smaller libraries, the library director usually does the PR as part of the overall job. The lack of attention paid to the smaller libraries is, therefore, not due to their librarians' commitment and skill in public relations, but rather the difficulty in isolating the PR process for examination.

PR Goals and Objectives

Stated goals and objectives, as well as policy statements, provide one way to determine a library's consciousness regarding public relations. In recent years public libraries have been given advice on specific public relations goals and objectives by the Planning Process document from the Public Library Association of ALA. The following is a sample:

> *Goal:* To improve the awareness of library services among county residents.
>
> *Objective:* To develop an aggressive publicity program aimed at awareness of library locations and services, with particular emphasis on the availability of nonprint materials and equipment, by 1981.
>
> *Objective:* To work with the school system to establish regular annual visits to the library by all elementary and junior high school students, by 1985.
>
> *Objective:* To increase the number of male users in branches by 10 per cent per year over the five-year period.[6]

Some libraries had written goals and objectives related to public relations prior to the issue of this document, but a surprising number did not have them as of 1980. (See Appendix for information on a survey of the Public Relations Section of the Library Administration and Management Association of ALA.) Only some one-third of the larger public libraries had PR goals and objectives, and even fewer of the smaller public libraries.

At the same time, academic libraries of all sizes reported few goals and objectives in this category. An examination of the ARL SPEC Kits dealing with goals and objectives did turn up some relating to public relations, but the "terrible term" itself was not used; in many cases even those goals and objectives more probably were not viewed as PR as well.

Some of the goals uncovered in academic libraries include:

> *From Texas A & M:* To promote research or innovative activities that will enhance the services and resources of the Texas A & M University Libraries or those of the larger library community.
>
> To create support for the University Libraries by promoting their services and resources.
>
> To develop constructive relationships with academic departments, the student body, and other units of the Uni-

versity, to help assure the development of the Libraries' resources and services consistent with the University's goals.

To develop constructive relationships with other libraries, professional associations, and cooperative organizations. [7]

From Massachusetts/Amherst: Actively promote the Library as a resource and interpret its collections to users, to assist them in utilizing the Library and in obtaining access to needed information located elsewhere.

Develop and utilize better ways of providing library resources and services based upon the analysis of user needs and the economical application of new technologies. [8]

From Cincinnati: To maintain close and meaningful working relationships with officials of the University and with academic departments and other official bodies to assure effective development of library services consistent with University objectives and programs. [9]

From Iowa State: Encourage increased dissemination of information concerning Library resources and services throughout the user community. [10]

From University of California/Riverside: The on-going development of and cooperation with an effective UCR Friends of the Library group. [11]

From Southern Illinois University: To cultivate the interests and contribution of people from the community and region in Library Affairs and to foster the development of endowments to support Library Affairs. [12]

From Notre Dame: The libraries shall maintain a dynamic and effective administrative structure to support the libraries' mission by promoting communication, assuring orderly planning, and implementing appropriate management techniques. It shall be a primary task of the library administration to work closely with other units in the University to develop and maintain a funding base through both internal and external sources adequate for the libraries' mission and objectives. [13]

From *University of California/Berkeley:* Promotion of facilities and services available to library users. [14]

From *Arizona State:* To promote effective communication with faculty: Reference librarians shall inform faculty members of the services and resources of the Reference department and encourage the use of these services and resources. [15]

These examples were selected because of their approach to academic library public relations. Emphasis is clearly on certain types of promotion, on target groups and on the survey technique for acquiring feedback.

School libraries, as part of larger school districts, often have the benefit of goals and objectives established for the larger unit, which can in turn be translated into more specific school library goals/objectives. For example, the ABC School District in California has as a goal, "Assure that the publics within the district have full access to information concerning programs and policies which concern them." Another goal is to "determine the public's reaction to the policies and programs anticipated or now carried out in the District." The final goal is to "create and maintain an atmosphere of mutual understanding and respect for children and adults residing, studying or employed within the ABC Unified School District."[16] These goals have clear implications for the libraries within the district's schools.

Another reflection of library philosophy regarding public relations is to be found in an agency's operating policies. For example, the Minneapolis Public Library has numerous policies in the PR areas, such as communication with the public, advertising in the library, elections and political activity, news releases, appearances, interviews and performances, library board meetings, citizen involvement, defense of personnel in civil actions, complaints concerning library personnel, gifts to library personnel, solicitations and sales in the library, community use of library meeting rooms, rules of conduct, research and study programs, and membership in area, state, regional and national associations. This list should not be considered a definitive one, since the policies of this and other libraries are constantly changing and redefined according to their goals and objectives.

Planned Programs of PR

Since goals and objectives, as well as policies, are often part of a larger plan, it might appear that most libraries don't have public relations plans. The actuality, though, may be that such libraries don't have formalized written plans for public relations, with specified goals and objectives for that particular function. When one inquires about plans for PR, librarians seem to be more positive in their responses. In the 1980 survey of PR/LAMA/ALA membership, 33.8 per cent of the respondents replied positively to the question, "Does your library have a planned program in public relations?" With public libraries, the larger the library, the greater likelihood that it had a PR plan. Unless things have changed radically since that 1980 survey, most libraries still do not have planned programs of public relations.

Library PR Budgets and Funding

Some librarians have long argued for separate PR budgets, suggesting that these budgets should be from two to ten per cent of the agency's total expenditures. Libraries responsible for all library promotion activities need higher PR budgets than those associated with larger systems, which may provide less expensive, or sometimes "free," promotion materials for their member libraries. [17] The 1980 survey revealed that most libraries did not have separate PR budgets, and of those willing to estimate a figure, more than half guessed that only one per cent or less of the library's money was spent on public relations. This is a depressing state of affairs, especially in light of studies that have shown a direct relationship between public relations activities and total financial support.[18]

Library Public Relations Staffing

With such evidence of a lack of planned programs, one might wonder whether those who are responsible for library planning and operations are aware of public relations at all. Yet, as K. C. Harrison suggests, "Perhaps it is only when one becomes a chief librarian or a director of libraries that the fullest appreciation of PR and its range and influence is attained."[19] One might conclude, nevertheless, that the directors of many libraries are so busy practicing PR that they don't have time to set up programs, define goals and objectives, or allocate specific PR budgets.

The library administrator should at least be aware of public relations, since it is a management function, as Sarah Wallace stated so well in 1963:

> Although public relations is the responsibility of everyone on the staff, everyone on the board, and all interested citizens, the direction of the PR program, if it is to create a unified, favorable and cohesive image, must follow a definite pattern. This can only be done if the program is managed by one qualified director and aimed toward one goal.[20]

Since it is a management function, in most libraries public relations should be handled by the director or by someone close to the top who is in constant contact with the director.

In reality one finds many patterns in the actual handling of a library's public relations. The director or assistant director, to be sure, may be responsible, but it is often merely a part-time assignment for some person on the library staff, sometimes a professional, sometimes not. A board member may take on the responsibility, or, in some cases, outside consultants or firms are hired to do the library's PR. Among these different approaches to getting the job done, some are less than adequate but there is no one way that is best. [21]

The reason why the person responsible for carrying out the day-to-day tasks of public relations in a library should be in a direct reporting relationship to the director (if it is not the director personally who does the job) is that easy access to the top is necessary to facilitate checking on facts for accuracy, to arrange community contacts, and to gain prompt action when it is needed. An individual with a split assignment, such as a children's librarian who is charged with doing the library's PR on a half-time basis, should report directly to the director for that portion of the job that deals with PR. Public relations must operate with the full knowledge and approval of top management if it is to be effective.

Among the components of the professional PR person's job in a library are tasks that can be grouped into four general areas of responsibility: 1/ representing the library to its clientele, 2/ promoting the use of the library by publicizing its resources and services, 3/ maintaining awareness of all materials of interest to, or about, the library in the local, national, and professional media, and 4/ making arrangements for visitors to the library and use of library facilities. These four primary responsibilities are not necessarily what a library PR practitioner's job should be, but they represent the actuality in most library settings, based on a job/task analysis done some years ago. Tasks for technical public relations persons include: 1/ editorial functions, 2/ administrative functions (supervising mailings and scheduling rooms), and 3/ graphic functions. Clerical PR tasks include: 1/ compilation of a clipping file or scrapbook about the library, 2/ maintenance of an archive of all material printed by the library, 3/ maintenance of mailing lists for library publications, 4/ maintenance of publicity materials stock, and 5/ arrangement of bulletin boards and displays. [22] The job descriptions for PR specialists in libraries vary, but most include some aspects of the four primary responsibilities listed above for professional-level tasks. These responsibilities are still quite narrow, and it is to be hoped that increased awareness of the importance of PR will result in broadening the responsibilities of the PR person's job.

Professional Librarian or Professional Publicist?

There is some difference of opinion about the qualifications required by the person who does library PR. Should that person be a librarian with PR skills, or a professional publicist (someone trained in public relations, marketing, journalism, etc.) who is sympathetic to the library's goals and objectives? The ideal, of course, is an individual with training in both librarianship and public relations, but this rarely happens unless the individual hired for a library PR position is equipped with one and dedicated enough to acquire training (and perhaps a degree) in the other. Some individuals with PR training have said that a library degree is helpful, not just for personal knowledge, but to provide "legitimate" credentials in the eyes of other librarians. It may be that librarians feel that the kind of commitment to the profession that is symbolized by a library degree is necessary to do the job with dedication, or that they are suspicious about someone whose first career loyalty is to a field other than librarianship.

On the other hand, some librarians seem to have increasing respect for the validity of other than library qualifications for the practice of some phases of library activity. In the 1980 survey, more than half the respondents said they felt some education in the various areas of promotion was necessary in order to do the PR job, and over three-fourths felt that library education was unnecessary.

Titles and Names

One interesting aspect of library public relations is its rare isolation as an activity for an individual within many libraries. This may be partly due to the names employed by libraries through the years to describe PR (and related) functions. Certain descriptive phrases seem to go through cycles of popularity, and one can see how different libraries view a particular function by the title they select for it.

An examination of the 37th edition of the *American Library*

Directory shows the variety of the terms used to describe public relations. In a simple check of each State's largest municipal public library, it was found that community services was the preferred title in 12 of the 23 libraries with clear designations in this area. Other terms used include public relations, public information, marketing, and community relations. In the PR/LAMA/ALA survey, in which responses came from librarians in all types of libraries, 42.7 per cent said that the preferred name in their libraries was public relations. Much less frequently used were publicity, public information, community relations, and community services.

A check of larger university libraries reveals a different story. Taking the current membership of the Association of Research Libraries and looking in the *American Library Directory* for the titles of individuals charged with the PR function in each of those libraries, one finds that only a few have any listing in this area. One example is a public affairs services department at UCLA. It can only be assumed that public-relations activities are not centered in one office or person, and that various functions have been split among public services, the director's office and someone (often the rare books or special collections librarian) serving as liaison for a Friends group.

In the 1980 survey, most respondents who were responsible for their libraries' public relations had written job descriptions. This may be because the libraries which have delineated a separate PR function tend to be larger in size, and more likely to have job descriptions for *all* staff members.

References

1. Frederick Glazer. "Selling the Library," *Library Journal* 99 (1 June 1974): 1518.

2. Arthur Curley. "Viewpoint: Service with a Snarl," *Library Journal* 97 (15 May 1972): 1785.

3. John Berry. "Rose-Colored Glasses," *Library Journal* 94 (15 October 1969): 3589.

4. Frank Capra. *It's a Wonderful Life*. Liberties Film, Produced by RKO, 1946.

5. O. B. Hardison, Jr. "The Ivory Tower in the Arena: Research Libraries and Public Outreach," *Wilson Library Bulletin* 53 (January 1979): 383. Dr. Hardison, in this article and in the original talk presented at the Southeastern Library conference in New Orleans in the Fall of 1978, never mentioned the term "public relations."

6. Vernon E. Palmour, Marcia C. Bellasi and Nancy DeWarth. *A Planning Process for Public Libraries*. Chicago, American Library Association, 1980, p. 246.

7. Office of Management Studies, Association of Research Libraries. *SPEC Kit #58: Goals and Objectives*. Washington, D.C., The Association, October 1979, p. 57–58.

8. *Ibid.*, p. 59.

9. *Ibid.*, p. 63.

10. *Ibid.*, p. 65.

11. *Ibid.*, p. 66.

12. *Ibid.*, p. 70.

13. *Ibid.*, p. 76.

14. Office of Management Studies, Association of Research Libraries. *SPEC Kit #84: Public Services Goals and Objectives in ARL Libraries*. Washington, D.C., The Association, May 1982, p. 43.

15. *Ibid.*, p. 83.

16. Dorothy Dubia. "Developing Goals, Planning, and Implementing a Positive PR Program," *Thrust—for Education Leadership* 3 (October 1973): 6.

17. Alice Norton. "Public Relations for Libraries," *Library Administration Division Newsletter* 3 (June 1977): 2.

18. For example: Patricia Berger. "An Investigation of the Relationship between Public Relations Activities and Budget Allocation in Public Libraries," *Information Processing & Management* 15 (1979): 179–93. And: E. Oakes. "An Investigation of the Relationship between Library Promotion Activities and Tax Support in Medium Sized Libraries in California." M.S., University of Southern California, 1971.

19. K. C. Harrison. *Public Relations for Libraries.* London, Andrew Deutsch, 1973, p. 9.

20. Sarah Wallace. "Public Relations: A Three-Way Definition," *Wilson Library Bulletin* 37 (March 1963): 558.

21. Sue Fontaine. "PR Tick/Click: A Report to the Council on Library Resources." Chicago, American Library Association, 1976.

22. Myrl Ricking and Robert E. Booth. *Personnel Utilization in Libraries: A Systems Approach.* Chicago, American Library Association, 1974, pp. 66–67.

VII LIBRARY MARKETING AND PR PROMOTION TECHNIQUES

THE PROJECTION of a positive institutional image is vital for the support and growth of organizations. A commercial enterprise is concerned with its image because it reflects upon the product and/or service the enterprise is selling. Nonprofit, service-oriented and other organizations dependent upon public support for capital and operating funds are necessarily even more concerned with their image, whatever their services and products.

Cutlip and Center, authors of a standard textbook on public relations, suggest that there are four "P's" involved in getting individuals to do what is wanted:

1/ Purchase, which means the actual buying of a product or service wanted.
2/ Patronage, which means trading off one item or favor for another.
3/ Pressure, which means that not supporting an idea will result in punishment of some sort.
4/ Persuasion, which means changing attitudes and therefore behavior to achieve the desired action. [1]

At first glance it would seem that the fourth of these items, persuasion, is the only one which has any application to library use. It is possible to think of applications for the others, such as punishment—the student not using the library might receive a low grade on a term paper—but persuasion certainly seems to be the most appropriate approach.

Service, nonprofit organizations often sadly discover that their services, materials, and programs are not clearly identified or understood by many individuals, yet the survival of the organization is really dependent upon general impressions and attitudes. "There may have been a time when good works spoke for themselves, but that day is far gone," said the Director of Program Support for the Boy Scouts of America.[2] This statement is applicable to many, if not all, nonprofit organizations, including libraries. To be acknowledged as an organization which does good does not mean that financial support will automatically follow.

How the image of an organization is projected, how public opinion and group attitudes are influenced, involves a number of public relations and marketing techniques. These techniques are not necessarily the province of specialists; many are easily employed by various staff members. It is these techniques as a group, rather than as single activities, that provide the basis for a sound public relations and marketing program.

By viewing these techniques within the framework of three different kinds of communication, it is possible to demonstrate certain similarities and distinctions among them. These three kinds of communication are 1/ communication which is printed and intended for large audiences; 2/ communication which involves spoken delivery and is intended for large groups; and 3/ communication that is both written and oral, but intended for one-to-one or small-group contact. There are other ways to group the various techniques, of course, but this method reveals certain commonalities which help show why the techniques involved are valid and useful PR and marketing techniques.

Printed, Mass Communication

Communication directed at large groups of the public by an organization includes a variety of tried-and-true, traditional techniques, such as news (press) releases, newsletters, annual reports, pamphlets, books, brochures, posters, signs, bill-boards, displays, slogan buttons, flyers and broadsides, as well as give-away gimmicks, such as T-shirts, balloons, and the like. The major element in all of these is the same: a clear, concise message that is designed to be read and understood. According to Raymond A. Bauer:

> Better educated people, and presumably more intelligent peo-
> ple prefer print media more than do lesser educated people.
> Better educated people retain more of the information trans-
> mitted in a communication, but they are not necessarily easier
> (or as easy) to shift from one attitudinal position to another.
> Better educated people also prefer more complex and sophisti-
> cated arguments.[3]

One might conclude from this that libraries, which provide print materials as one of their more traditional and basic ser-vices, are most likely to use printed PR materials to communi-cate with their presumably intelligent users. Obviously, one needs to remember that, even among library patrons, there are individuals who do not necessarily prefer print materials and are not always best communicated with in print format.

A definite advantage of printed media is that they are more permanent, and certainly last longer, than the majority of other forms of communication. A printed message goes not only to the individuals to whom it is disseminated originally, but may well be passed on to others beyond the first contact group. Some of the techniques mentioned above—buttons, posters and T-shirts—are meant to be viewed by a large au-dience over a lengthy period of time. In addition, the wearing of a button, the holding of a balloon, or the carrying of an imprinted shopping bag implies a kind of personal endorse-ment by the individual, which is another aspect of commu-nication and promotion. Also possible with this technique are more blatant appeals, such as the obvious sexual one of a well-endowed female in a tight t-shirt emblazoned with a motto.[4]

Of the three types of communication, what we are discuss-ing here is in most cases one-way communication. Two-way communication may be initiated later, depending on the inclination of the receiver, but usually it is very difficult to evaluate in a quantitative fashion.[5] In most cases, this type of communication is meant to draw attention. It is not the sole, or even the most important, communication technique for an organization's PR/marketing process.

Another advantage of print format is its more measured preparation before actual distribution. Any number of individuals can preview the copy and make suggestions. Its final production may involve yet more people, and this in turn provides additional interest in the message. On the other hand, it is sometimes difficult to implement printed messages quickly, and personality conflicts can erupt over seemingly simple information to be sent out in the name of the organization. Some people take the opportunity to do some empire building within the organization, with claims that they, and only they, can give final approval for certain printed communications.

An obvious disadvantage of printed messages is the lack of control over the individual pieces once they leave the organization. Outdated or incorrect material can prove to be a source of embarrassment for a longer period of time than is true with some other forms of communication. Printed messages cannot practically be manufactured for self-destruction at a predetermined time, and the advantage of long life for this type of communication may in fact turn into a disadvantage.

Another disadvantage of printed formats is the lack of a personal touch. Since in most cases a large audience is targeted to receive the message, the wording of the message will often be impersonal. One may intend a message which "hits home" with each individual receiver, but bulk mailings often lack that genuine, this-is-meant-for-you-alone feeling. This is no doubt why so many advertising messages are phrased in the second person, for the pronoun "you" may be interpreted in a personal way by the receiver.

What to write and how to write print messages that will be read by the right people and understood by most of them, that will sway the attitudes and resulting actions of many, and provide new, continued and strengthened support for an organization and its services are important skills for those involved in PR and marketing. David Ogilvy, a well-known advertising specialist, includes a chapter of advice on writing advertising copy in his book, *Confessions of an Advertising Man*. Two points from that chapter are good advice for all writers:

1/ Don't beat about the bush—go straight to the point. Avoid analogies of the "just so, so too" variety. Dr. Gallup has demonstrated that these two-stage arguments are generally misunderstood.

2/ Avoid superlatives, generalizations, and platitudes. Be specific and factual. Be enthusiastic, friendly, and memorable. Don't be a bore. Tell the truth, but make the truth fascinating.[6]

Verbal and Visual Mass Communication

Verbal and visual mass communication includes the newer forms of electronic communication, radio and television, and speeches and presentations, either audio-visual or live, to groups. The importance of *how* the message is communicated is most apparent here, partly because of the possibility of using a wide variety of formats:

All media work us over completely. They are so pervasive in their personal, political, economic, aesthetic, psychological, moral, ethical and social consequences that they leave no part of us untouched, unaffected, unaltered. The medium is the massage. Any understanding of social and cultural change is impossible without a knowledge of the way media work as environments. All media are extensions of some human faculty—psychic or physical.[7]

Marshall McLuhan's words are now well known and accepted by many. The appeal of audio-visual formats is obvious. The messages sent through electronic formats not only reach large numbers of people, but audiences which are not necessarily grouped according to social class.

Electronic methods of communication seem to have the greatest appeal to most people, and also have the physical potential to reach more people than is possible using other methods. Also, there is greatly increased potential for enhancing a message and its impact in ways that increase the chances of attracting listeners, holding their interest and convincing them that the message is one they should accept. Sound effects, background music, visual excitement and dramatic interpretation are but a few of the added weapons available with this style of communication. However, although there are often advantages in directing messages through more than one of the human senses simultaneously, there is also greater potential for misunderstanding or misfiring in the complex process of communication and information transfer when visual is added to audio impact (or vice versa), smell added to visual, and so on.

There are two types of situations in which messages may be received. When a printed format is used, the receiver is generally a person alone, who, although he/she may not be the only one to receive the same printed message, reads that message by himself or herself. When a printed message is read aloud by one person to another, or to a group, this is verbal rather than written mass communication. Most written messages are received and read by individuals in a singular fashion. With verbal and visual mass communication, however, there are two ways in which the message may be received: one is singular, as with written communication—many people, for example, listen to radio or watch television alone. The same message, however, may also be received by an assembled group of people, and one then needs to consider the implications of group attitudes and reactions.[8]

When a message is sent and received is important, but timing, with either printed or some audio-visual formats, cannot always be predetermined. Public service announcements on radio may be aired at any time, and a printed annual report may be glanced at immediately after receipt or much later. Only with in-person speeches and presentations can the timing of the message and its receipt be determined with any degree of certainty.

Most messages are sent with a view to their receipt at an optimal time, to ensure acceptance by the receiver. When a message is received can determine how the receiver will react to it. The action resulting from the receiver's perception of the message is the crux of the matter. With commercial messages, timing is not always as critical, since purchase at any time is usually deemed a success. But support for a political issue after an election is usually fruitless, as is sincere but apathetic concern for community agencies in need of funds. When a message is received may actually dictate when the message is reacted to, and this may determine the success or failure of the appeal.

Another fact to consider in using electronic and audiovisual presentations is the present level of sophistication and the high expectations of many people, and the likelihood of their rejecting a message on the grounds of amateurish presentation. Their interest may well focus on technical problems rather than on the message itself, or worse, they may feel that shoddy or sloppy delivery is representative of a shoddy or sloppy organization. Beyond the technical considerations, the impact of a message may be ruined by tripping up over some small, overlooked detail. Vance Packard's classic, *The Hidden Persuaders*, tells the story of the problems of manufacturer trying to promote a self-defrosting refrigerator:

> In the ad in print and on TV, the refrigerator was shown with the door wide open, unattended. The Institute for Motivational Research, in talking to housewives who had seen this ad, found what it believed to be the reason for their failing to try to buy the wonderful product. It found that all the message about the merits of automatic defrosting had gone right past the women, unheeded. They couldn't take their eyes off that wide-open refrigerator and wondered uneasily what kind of housekeeper would be so careless in wasting electricity and letting food spoil.[9]

The print format is very much with us, and if it is true that it is the medium which most appeals to the intelligentsia, it cannot be considered unsophisticated. Electronic and audio-visual presentations, however, need to be produced not with the idea that the intended audience is the great "unwashed," but that today's media-oriented audiences have a lot of experience, and hence sophistication, in listening to, watching, and accepting various messages.

Communication on a One-to-One Basis

One-to-one communication is a third way of conveying messages. This kind of communication may be written, spoken, or conveyed through sign/body language, but it differs from the two previous communication styles in that it is designed and produced particularly for a specific recipient. Techniques include the use of conversation (telephone and in person), letters, memoranda, tape cassettes, and the organization grapevine. This style is more often spontaneous and informal than the communication methods discussed previously.

This does not mean, however, that this type of public relations requires less planning and thought. It is often necessary to communicate effectively and convincingly with one person in order to produce positive public relations results. Interpersonal communication and relationships can be the most crucial aspects of an organization's public relations program, because, as with all plans, programs, and processes, it is the people doing the job who have the power to control the end product. Less attention should not be devoted to this type of communication merely because fewer people receive the message. Interpersonal communication should be considered of utmost importance: it is fundamental in convincing key people to help get a desired result.

An important aspect of this style of communication is the high potential for feedback based on immediate reactions. It is also the easiest of the three styles of communication to evaluate in terms of its success or failure. Small group contacts have similar advantages.

This process has been described in clinical terms:

> Clinically, a person who is participating in a well-functioning network is characterized by the presence of an operational attitude—curiosity, and eagerness to find out what the effects

of a statement or an action may have been. Such a person usually considers other individuals and groups in terms of whether or not they will be able to cope with the effects of a projected statement or an anticipated action. Such a person incessantly works toward improvement of the facilities for feedback. He asks others for suggestions and incorporates these into his new plans. [10]

Personality and character are very important factors in interpersonal communication. Those who are insecure, easily threatened, or have an inordinate need for ego stroking are unlikely to function as good communicators and/or public relations specialists. Such individuals really only want positive feedback, and their need for reinforcement overpowers any real desire to know and understand other people's reactions and attitudes. Interaction with direct, honest communicators is avoided, or, if it cannot be, the insecure person may rush to the offensive in an attempt to discredit feedback before it is ever delivered. In this manner the individual uneasy about his or her communication and interpersonal skills can avoid any sort of negative feedback.

This style of communication is particularly important in internal public relations. Much communication, formal and informal, in organizations is conducted on a one-to-one basis. This is significant in the overall public relations process because of the role everyone in the organization must play. For goals and objectives to be reached, there must be effective internal organizational communication, so that all employees understand and work toward accomplishment of the same ends. Internal conflicts between individuals and departments should be kept in perspective, at least as far as the PR /marketing program is concerned; the organization's aims can and should be supported in spite of any petty quarrels and rivalries.

Library Promotion

Most emphasis in library public relations and marketing has been on the techniques of promotion, involving principally one-way communication. These techniques are clearly very important in telling the library story and projecting a positive image, but librarians have allowed their interest in this phase of PR/marketing to become too predominant. It is important to remember that unless publicity techniques are used as part of a thoughtful overall marketing plan, they will probably not achieve the desired results.

In some cases the present emphasis has been caused because librarians not trained in publicity techniques have had to learn new basic skills in order to carry out library publicity. It is only natural to want to apply those new skills to specific projects, but it is unfortunate sight is lost of the basic reason for doing the job in the first place. It is too easy to become process-oriented and forget the end product—an improved image for the library. There is an unquestionable attraction in viewing a final physical product, such as an attractive newsletter or annual report, and librarians sometimes think more about the means of conveying their message than about the less tangible, long-range results.

Nevertheless, publicity items do play a part in the total library PR/marketing program, and consideration needs to be given to some of the more commonly used and successful approaches. Most of the types of publicity described here have multiple purposes, including imparting specific information, and are not done solely to promote the library. Whatever other reasons there may be for the production of these publicity items, however, all of them do contribute to the overall image projected by the library.

News Releases

A basic promotion tool is the news release, sometimes called a press release. This is the means by which newsworthy items of information are sent to the mass media, whether of past events or of forthcoming programs. Certain precise journalistic rules govern the writing of good news releases, which are usually fairly brief and factual. Libraries use news releases to announce programs and new services, personnel changes, budget increases or decreases, awards and gifts, and such milestone events as acquisition of the library's millionth book.

Releases are generally used to report positive news, although they can be used to alert the public to problems and concerns. This is not the correct format for feature stories in newspapers and local magazines. These should be worked out with appropriate editors before going into final copy. News releases are a quick, convenient way to let the public know what's happening, but good judgment should be exercised in sending them out; blitzing the local media with too many news releases about minor events will result in few of them being used.

Some librarians, particularly in smaller communities where newspapers are eager for stories about the library, are able to write often, sometimes in the form of weekly columns about library activities. Even simple lists of the new books that have come in and are ready for use are acceptable, although this is probably not the best use the library can make of generously provided space. In larger communities it is somewhat more difficult to obtain newspaper space, other than in smaller circulation suburban papers, but even in these settings newspaper editors are generally willing to consider feature stories about the library.

Library Publications

Libraries issue a number of different publications, and for various reasons, including: 1/ promotion of the library and its services, 2/ promotion of specific services, programs and/or library materials, 3/ provision of community information, 4/ encouraging library use, 5/ fundraising, and 6/ reporting.[11] Libraries should have policies governing their publications, and detailing specifically the types of publications to be issued, who they are intended for, and who is responsible for them.[12] Library publications are often simple affairs, such as one-page pathfinders, booklets on how to use the library, bookmarks, and the like. This simplicity is one reason why there is often no library policy guiding their initiation, production, and distribution, which can result in confusion and unhappy PR mistakes. Clarity of purpose and procedure is necessary if the library's printed promotion pieces are to be used effectively.

Booklists

A traditional favorite among library handouts is the booklist, or bibliography, of suggested readings on a certain subject. In recent years many of these have broadened in scope to include nonprint and other library materials. The booklist is both a popular and a useful tool, particularly when issued in the form of the traditional bookmark and/or simple printed handout. But, as with so many library promotion techniques, despite its continued success it is viewed as somewhat suspect, merely because it's been around for so long. Librarians, unfortunately, tend to think that promotion ideas need to be new and different in order to be successful.

Booklists are still an effective technique, however, and one with a sound purpose. Booklists draw attention to titles which are not always well known. They publicize unusual subjects, encourage exploration of new subjects and old favorites, and provide people, particularly children, with a souvenir of their trip to the library. They discourage dog-earing the pages of library books, and they can be passed along from one person to another, perhaps encouraging someone new to come to the library. Lists can provide a framework for a booktalk in classrooms and at community group meetings. They can be part of a library display, or a simple beginning of bibliographic instruction. They provide one more place to show the library's name, location, and hours of service.

The booklist's value is often overlooked because it seems so obvious. Even as librarians often neglect to mention that programs and services of the public library are "free," so they often forget the tried-and-true values of the ubiquitous booklist. Even in today's world of online searches, the simple printed booklist still has value: it is relatively inexpensive, easy to compile, and liked by many people. As long as there are books, there should be library booklists.

In academic and research libraries booklists are generally called bibliographies, but they serve the same basic purpose as in other types of libraries—to draw attention to material that may be of use, or interest, to the potential reader.

Library Guides and Handbooks

Printed guides and handbooks remain popular with library users even though many librarians now favor audio-visual presentations and other newer methods. Whatever the format a key question is the amount of information to be provided, and there is still no consensus on this matter. In general, guides provide information about the library and the rules for its use, and handbooks provide information about library materials and how to use them. Bibliographic instruction is currently in vogue as another way to give library users what they need to know in order to utilize the library effectively and efficiently.

The traditional printed format for guides and handbooks continues to be popular for several reasons. It has been stated earlier that more educated people prefer print as a communication medium. Also, a printed guide or handbook can be picked up and read at any time and any place. This can be done without the need for an appointment with a specialist or use of audio-visual hardware. A single item can be checked more quickly for a needed piece of information than playing through an entire tape. Although many libraries have added other methods of providing library guidance and bibliographic instruction, the printed guide and/or handbook remains in use because it is preferred by many users.

It is sometimes difficult to differentiate between a guide and a handbook, since the basic functions may be merged. This is most common in academic libraries. Guides and/or handbooks are usually distributed free and are frequently the most expensive promotion pieces used by academic libraries.

There are some difficulties which arise in the preparation of guides and handbooks. One obviously relates to how much information to provide, or—to put it another way—how can enough information be provided without overwhelming the reader? Too much information can be as bad as too little, and extraneous material may serve only to bore, confuse, or even alienate the library user. The interest in these problems is evidenced by the number of publications on educating the library user, such as those edited by John Lubans. There are a number of clearinghouses located in regional centers where sample materials developed by different libraries can be examined.

Annual Reports

Annual reports come usually in two different formats in most libraries. There are reports of an official nature which are produced by the overwhelming majority of all types of libraries in response to higher authority. These are usually prepared according to a prescribed format and tend to be lengthy, filled with statistics and detailed financial information. The other kind of annual report is a summary version of the official one and is prepared for a larger audience, library users for example. These are not requested (or required by law), but are generally produced because of their value in showing a wider audience what the library has done with its budget over the past year. In other words, it provides an opportunity to demonstrate library accountability.

Public librarians have long recognized the value of the summary annual report for a larger audience, and now other types of libraries are adopting this form of promotion. University libraries, for example, may provide handsome annual reports for their Friends of the Library groups and donors to special collections, and these are also often distributed to potential donors. School librarians will sometimes distribute statistical reports to teachers in their schools in order to show to what extent the library is being used. Special librarians combine annual reports with announcements of available services to encourage wider use of their collections and services. Information specialists distribute reports on popular search topics to inspire further use.

The annual report can be more than a mere annual accounting. It can also be used to emphasize certain figures and draw attention to library needs. It is a time-honored way to attract attention and, if nothing else, can often be the means to obtain a solid, factual newspaper account of the library's state-of-affairs.

An essential factor in preparing an annual report is involvement of the staff in compiling facts and statistics for inclusion. These data can be pulled from departmental annual reports or monthly reports to supervisors, program and service evaluations, or some may be solicited specifically for the library's annual report. In compiling an annual report it is apparent that "there are individual winners; and no individual losers. All must cooperate so that nothing won't be the result."[14]

Library Newsletters

Newsletters, sometimes called house organs, are useful publications, particularly for libraries with large staff and/or patron groups. Ideally, they should be issued frequently, or at least regularly, in an attractive format with useful, mostly shorter items of interest. The library newsletter has all the advantages and disadvantages of printed communication, the ability to provide quick and frequent communication with a predetermined, specific audience, generally controlled by means of a mailing/distribution list. There is the further advantage that newsletters can be relatively inexpensive; a glossy presentation is usually not necessary, expected, or even particularly desirable. Newsletters also make possible a quick, printed record of official notification, of policy changes, for example. Disadvantages primarily center on the assessment of need, since libraries do not necessarily need this particular means of promotion and/or communication. Information which might go into a newsletter might just as easily in some settings be disseminated by means of an occasional memorandum. A newsletter can become a tedious chore for its editor, a needless expense for the library, and, all too often, may be left unread by its intended audience.

Newsletters must be current and honest. Old news is cold news, and using a newsletter as a "puff-sheet" merely diminishes its impact. A conscientious attempt should be made to include library staff in the gathering of items for the newsletter, as well as in seeking feedback on the newsletter.

There are two common kinds of newsletters in libraries: the staff newsletter and the newsletter aimed at such outside audiences as library patrons, the business community, a library friends group, teachers, or other special groups. Most libraries have found it difficult, impractical, and poor communication practice to try to make one newsletter do the job of reaching both internal staff and outside groups. The need to match information carefully with the intended group is the first principle of good communication. What is of interest and importance to one group, such as the library staff, will not in many cases be of interest and importance to outside groups. The library staff, however, will want to see copies of newsletters prepared for outside groups and may help in the preparation, but the information there should not appear as news to staff. Libraries of a reasonable size should probably consider having both types of newsletters.

Newsletters are popular in academic and special libraries, as well as in public libraries, and are frequently used to draw attention to new or special materials, changes in library rules, personnel changes, and special events. In an academic community newsletters may be directed toward the faculty and/or the library staff. A special newsletter might well be developed for a friends group. In special libraries, all company employees might receive a general newsletter, or one may be directed more selectively to department heads. Public libraries usually have special mailing lists for their newsletters for the wider community, covering such groups as city leaders, persons engaged in business, friends, community leaders, teachers, or other targeted groups. School libraries are likely to have a newsletter for the administration and teachers, and possibly for students and/or their parents as well.

Staff newsletters involve additional decisions, which may even result in further newsletter categories. A strong staff association or union will probably want to produce its own association or union newsletter, in addition to that produced by the library administration. The source of the information in a newsletter, obviously, must be very clear. Combined or cooperative efforts, using devices such as alternating issues or devoting a page of space to "the other side," are rarely successful. In large part this is because of staff suspicions about administrative domination of any such cooperative ventures. The impact of the news is thereby undermined; rather than the message being accepted for what is, there is a tendency to speculate on motivations or even the possibility of administrative conspiracies.

Staff newsletters produced by the library administration need to feature news in the real sense, and not be vehicles for expounding administrative orders and dicta. They should deal with matters of concern to the staff, including items under consideration on which feedback from staff is desired. Issues and problems can be explored and explained. Staff openings can be advertised first in the newsletter, and new policies and policy changes announced. Administratively sponsored newsletters for the library staff tend to be crisper in tone than those sponsored by staff associations. An official aura is appropriate, since such newsletters are a means of official communication between the administration and the staff.

An ARL SPEC Kit dealing with internal communication outlines newsletter possibilities:

> Newsletters can fulfill a number of functions. They can describe the objectives of the library and encourage staff involvement in helping achieve the objectives. They can describe and explain operating policies and practices, and alert the staff to changes before they occur. They can provide news of current activities of the library and the environment in which it operates, and they can point out accomplishments of the library as a whole and of individual staff members.[15]

In a survey by ALA's Public Relations Section of LAMA, nearly half of the respondents reported that newsletters were used to communicate with staff. The larger libraries, of course, had a higher positive response. Probably more libraries have staff newsletters than newsletters for outside groups, perhaps because of the higher production costs involved in external communication.

Staff newsletters produced by staff associations or unions are often chattier and include more personal information. Recipes, free classifieds for staff and also matters of professional concern to the group, written from a staff viewpoint, are often featured. They are friendlier in tone than most administratively-sponsored newsletters. Communication among peers is usually freer and more open than communication downward from a higher authority.

Library Posters

Library posters are used for display and to draw attention to materials, services, and events both inside and outside the library. They are produced in an array of sizes, colors, and styles, and for a variety of purposes. The versatility of the poster is in part responsible for its long popularity, and the appeal of posters as an art form makes them an admirable publicity vehicle for libraries.

As with any graphic form of communication, a successful poster is eye-catching, attractive, simple, readable and understandable. Some libraries produce their own posters, but there are a number of different sources from which posters may be purchased or obtained free. These include the American Library Association and the Children's Book Council, as well as such commercial poster makers as Upstart Library Promotionals. State libraries and state library associations also sometimes provide posters, and a good source for free posters is publishers, especially those of children's books, who often distribute posters at library conferences advertising various books.

Library Logos

A library logo is an identifying graphic symbol. In the commercial world, logos are usually referred to as trademarks and are considered part of a company's visual image. Such logos, or trademarks, are the descendants of brands used to signify ownership but they have since evolved into symbols for a company or organization and as reminders of a company's products. In the case of libraries, a logo can be used as a symbol for the library itself, or as a graphic illustration of the materials and services of the library.

Trademark design has become increasingly sophisticated in recent times.[16] The U.S. Trademark Association has suggested a number of desirable characteristics of a trademark: brevity, easy to remember, easily readable and speakable, easily adapted to any medium, no unpleasant connotations, suitable for export, lends itself to pictorialization and subtlety.[17] An example of a very successful trademark is the Nabisco Company's red triangle on the upper left corner of every product it puts out. Because of its consistent use over the years (unlike NBC's peacock, which seems to come and go)[18] and continued consumer exposure to it through advertising, this trademark is very effective.

Efforts to modernize trademarks have sometimes succeeded, but in some cases commercial companies have found it advantageous to return to an older symbol. RCA, for example, tried dumping its famous dog and for a period depended purely on a modern, stylized depiction of its acronym. It became apparent, however, that in the minds of most consumers, the company was recognized first not by its initials but by the little dog with its ear cocked, listening to its master's voice. So the dog came back. An example of successful and consistent use of a trademark which has gone through gradual modernization is Morton's salt girl, who has been redrawn a number of times, but who has kept her umbrella, salt, and pouring rain.

Graphic symbols to communicate a message, such as the hammer and sickle of communism, sometimes work. In most cases, through, education as to what the symbol means is necessary. A marketing study discovered, for example, that nursery school children do not necessarily recognize the familiar skull and crossbones as a symbol for poison. Rather, the majority of children in the test saw it as a symbol for "pirate food."[19] Another example of this need for education in recognition are the symbols other countries use for basic services, such as a circle with a ring of shapes, used to designate a telephone in Brazil.

Conceptually, libraries have often had difficulty in obtaining effective logos. This has not discouraged them from trying, however, and many good logos have been developed. Among the concepts that have been incorporated are the stylized Lincoln hat and beard for the Springfield, Illinois, Public Library, the mighty river rippling down the center of a book for Memphis, and many examples of handsomely stylized books. Monograms, or initials, of library systems are common, as are drawings of the library building. Some libraries use more abstract symbols.

The primary purpose of the library logo is to serve as an identification mark for the library's external communications, on flyers and stationery, and on bookmobiles, signs, and exhibits. A library logo is most successful when it instantly means "library" to the majority of those who see it. David Ogilvy, discussing the importance of trademarks and the great need for brand identification, comments wryly:

When the client moans and sighs,
Make his logo twice the size.[20]

Successful organizations need to emphasize their identity with the public, and a logo is one way to do this. It indicates a pride of ownership.

Logo design is probably best done by a professional artist. Since a logo is (or should be) used for maximum exposure, its graphic appearance is vital to its success, both in attracting attention and in conveying a sense of quality about the organization it represents. A logo should look polished and pass every design test.

No real specifics can be given for good logo design. There are no simple rules to follow, although certain design styles become popular at different times. In 1962 the *Official Gazette* of the U.S. Patent Office reported that more trademarks were designed within circles than in any other shape (next highest was the rectangle).[21] Current use seems to favor the square. Psychologically, the circle is considered the most "perfect" shape but that does not mean it is necessarily best for a particular organization's identification.[22]

A logo can be used on all of the library's publications, including stationery, and often on signs, buildings or bookmobiles—anything that can be identified as associated with the library. It becomes a part of the library's overall image, part of the overall impression the library is trying to project.[23]

The national library symbol, or logo, adopted by ALA in 1982 is usually enclosed in a square, or rectangle. The design is of a stylized person reading a book and is done in blue on white (or vice versa) except when the logo is used as a highway sign; it must then be in green. Originally developed by the Western Maryland Public Libraries for system-wide use, the logo was chosen by ALA as a general symbol for libraries in the U.S. A number of individual libraries have used it as their own symbol.

Other countries have also adopted library logos, including the United Kingdom and the Federal Republic of Germany. The British logo, adopted in 1982. shows a block "L" hewn from a square. The German logo shows a series, or stack, of vee shapes, resembling the open pages of a book. (See Figure 2.)

Library Slogans

Slogans, or mottoes, have been used by companies or organizations for centuries. The word slogan is an adaptation from a Celtic word meaning "battle cry." The purpose of using a slogan is to inspire loyalty to a company or organization, as well as to encapsulate a basic idea which identifies the organization. "Be prepared!" is certainly recognized by most people as the slogan of the Boy Scouts, as is "Semper Fidelis" for the U.S. Marine Corps. Slogans are most often used on advertisements, posters, buttons, and other printed promotion pieces, as well as in media ads. Some commercial slogans have proved to be memorable, such as "Have you driven a Ford lately?" and "Things go better with Coke." Many fail to catch on.

Figure 2
Library logos: top, U.S.; center, the U.K.;
bottom, Federal Republic of Germany

In the modern commercial world there is growing confusion over the slogans used by various companies, partly because of the frequency with which they are changed and also because of the similarity between the slogans of different companies. It is sometimes difficult to figure out, from its slogan alone, what product or service a company offers.

Slogans have long been a part of library promotions, and particularly since the advent of National Library Week in the 1950s. In the early days of NLW, slogans were suggested by members of a citizens' committee, including some well-known advertising specialists, such as Bill Bernbach of Doyle, Dane and Bernbach. Every year a slogan was selected to be graphically expressed on posters and transformed into electronic messages for radio and television. Since those early days of slogan use, other library companies and associations have devised slogans for use in their promotion campaigns.

Determining the success of a slogan can be difficult, but slogans can be judged on the basis of three important factors: interest, distinctiveness, and believability. Interest is usually evoked by originality. What is there about the slogan that will attract interest from people—is it an attention-grabber? Distinctiveness also involves originality, but it really derives from the clarity of image promoted by the slogan. What image of the product or service immediately comes to mind when you hear the slogan? Believability relates to truth. Not all advertising slogans are totally honest, but they may still be believable in the sense that you believe what you want to hear. Do you nod in agreement when you hear the slogan?

One reason why it is difficult to gauge the success of slogans is that the public is generally exposed to them as part of an audio-visual experience. Some slogans have been more successfully conveyed visually by poster artists, others have been translated neatly into television messages. If one goes back to the three factors for slogan success—interest, distinctiveness, believability—it is possible to test individual slogans by assigning numerical values to the three factors as related to each slogan. Librarians find some slogans more effective than others. In workshop and class tests over a period of ten years, the author has found that one of the older ones, "Know What

You're Talking About—Read!" has tested out consistently well. An early Library Upstart slogan, "Get It at the Library," has also held up well through the years. In recent years, the slogan "A Nation of Readers," first developed by the Center for the Book at the Library of Congress, is liked by many librarians. Such analysis has not been tried directly with the public, although occasionally someone will react to a particular slogan positively or negatively, as when Jean Stafford wrote a piece for *The New Yorker* entitled "What the Heck is National Library Week?"[25]

One final observation on slogans in library promotion: in 1968 the National Library Week slogan was "Be All You Can Be—Read!" This is now being used (without the "read") by the U.S. Army for recruitment purposes.

Exhibits and Displays

Such special visual presentations as bulletin boards and exhibits/displays have been used for some years, both inside and outside the library, to draw attention to library materials, services, and programs. They range from simple bulletin boards to elaborate historical and art exhibits mounted in special exhibition galleries. Probably the best known displays in library history were those set up by Kate Copland in the windows of Baltimore's Enoch Pratt Free Library. They were designed to entice passers-by into the building. Today, displays are commonly accepted as useful promotion tools, because of their tested ability to attract people's interest. One study showed that students like exhibits better than bulletin boards,[26] and that there is value in introducing objects other than just library materials into displays.

Since most librarians are not Kate Coplands, there is often a reluctance to tackle large, imposing display cases. All too often the results are less than satisfactory, the displays cluttered and/or visually unorganized. But as with other forms of library promotion, guides on how to put up good displays are available, if professional artistic assistance cannot be hired.[27]

Public Service Announcements

Libraries, as well as other community, educational, and/or cultural organizations, rely on radio and television for exposure of special programs and promotion of materials and services. Air time for commercial advertising is expensive, and libraries generally seek categorization of their messages as public service announcements (PSAs). Radio and television stations are not required by federal regulations to broadcast PSAs, but it is a popular method used by many stations to prove that a community service has been provided when license renewal time comes.[28] Libraries can get their share of PSA time on both radio and television, and it is up to the local librarian to determine which stations are more inclined to provide this service.

The major disadvantage of PSAs is lack of control over when the message airs, since most radio and television stations are commercial and give preferential air time to advertisers who have paid for it, fitting PSAs into leftover periods. Some of these times may be desirable ones that no advertiser has purchased, and a good relationship with station managers is needed in order to find out about some of these prime-time openings. It is necessary, in any case, to develop spots according to the time specifications of the stations. It may be possible to get the one-minute spot right before the eight a.m. newscast, but spots specifically written for one minute must be provided.

Other electronic media opportunities include station editorials which may focus on the library, community calendars listing events going on in the community, regular news programs for big information items, and public affairs programs.[29]

FRIENDS and Friends

A powerful public relations tool for libraries is people themselves, those indivdiuals and groups who are favorably disposed toward the library. Such individuals may be willing to speak up in favor of the institution and are often willing to work on its behalf through Friends of the Library groups, advisory committees, concerned citizens, volunteers, and members of other groups interested in forming coalitions with the library to work for common goals.

Friends groups and individuals should never be shunted off in a corner so that the library administration and staff need not bother with them on a day-to-day basis; neglect will bring about waning interest or apathy. Friends should not be involved in what's going on only in times of trouble, or when the library wants their help. They should be involved as much as possible without interfering with the actual running of the library.

Library Friends are not always library users; they may well be supporters of the library's purpose without using the library's collections, services, and programs personally. They may have family members who are ardent library users, for example. Whatever the reason, library usage need not be the price of membership for a formal or informal library friends group.

Friends of the Library groups have been formally organized throughout the country since the 1920s. [30] There is now a national association for Friends, called Friends of Libraries USA (FOLUSA), which is affiliated with ALA. Friends groups have become more numerous in the past few decades, particularly in academic and research libraries, where they are seen as a valuable conduit for fund raising and establishing foundations. A survey of academic librarians in 1975 revealed that 55 per cent saw their friends groups primarily as aids in fund raising and developing support, as well as in providing advice to the library administration. Twenty-three per cent said that general support of the library was the primary objective for the group, yet only a very few said that fund raising was their sole objective. [31] In 1974 the clear focus of Friends groups was on financial support, collection development, and the stimulation of community support for the academic library. Included within these basic objectives are activities such as fund-raising programs, publications, building of special collections, regular meetings, community awareness and support for campaigns, lectures, and social events. [32] In public and school libraries, friends groups are often engaged in similar activities, as well as in organizing such activities as book fairs.

In addition to organized Friends groups, libraries have other supporters who serve the library as enthusiastic volunteers, and often act as informal spokespersons for the library. These people generate that valuable public-relations commodity, positive word-of-mouth publicity, which is difficult to measure but terribly important in building a good image of the library in its community. The library has many friends, and wise librarians keep them informed, communicate with them frequently, seek and listen to their ideas and opinions, and treat the friendships as a valuable library resource.

Presentations to Community Groups

In addition to the techniques described above, librarians engage in other types of public relations which might better be described as community relations. A common technique here includes talks (be they informal discussions or sophisticated media shows) to various groups in the library's community, often in places outside the library. These presentations usually describe the library and its services, and sometimes focus on a special part of the collection or a specific service which may be of particular interest to the community group being addressed. A presentation to a Lions' Club might well center on large print books and other library services for the blind because of that club's long involvement with fund raising for visual protection and assistance. A talk to school administrators might well concentrate on relations betwen school and public libraries and the primary functions of each. A special librarian might give a demonstration of new online data-base searching services to a group of scientists working for the corporation. Academic librarians are regularly involved in giving presentations about their libraries to groups of students and faculty.

Structured booktalks and story hours for children are another way for librarians to demonstrate the agency's collections by highlighting specific books and stories and whetting the audience's appetite for more. Booktalks are generally given to adults and young adults, either in the library or elsewhere; story hours for children are usually given in the library itself. Both of these are tested and true program activities in public and school libraries, although they are seldom used in academic or special libraries.

Classroom visits by librarians are another technique which has been used effectively through the years. Public librarians from the children's department often visit neighboring schools to describe the public library and invite children and their parents to come to the library. School librarians, of course, make classroom presentations in their own schools, and academic librarians may also visit classes to describe library services and collections.

A final form of presentations by librarians is the holding of receptions in the library for various groups, often including tours of the library. All types of libraries have found this simple approach to public relations to be a useful way to make new friends for the library.

Library Programs

Special programs (usually one-time offerings) are often used by librarians as another way to attract people to the library. The ultimate goal in providing these programs is to encourage new users of the library's services. Public libraries especially have used this promotion technique, employing a wide variety of programs, including lunch-time lectures, film series, and evening demonstrations devoted to high-interest topics. Some of these programs may be periodic in nature; for example, an annual book sale of duplicate gift books, a summer reading program for children, a term-paper clinic for new college students, or orientation to the library for new corporation employees. Others, though, will be one-shot programs, such as a bicycle safety program, a karate demonstration, or a slide show on a foreign country.

Some programs become so popular that they evolve into more regular library services. A regular booktalk at lunch hour for working people in the neighborhood, a preschool story hour, or an investors' club may all result from single, successful programs. Those events that work can often be easily converted into regular services. The difficulty comes in the periodic evaluation of these program-generated services, particularly when the time comes to give serious consideration to discontinuation. Librarians, like the rest of the human race, find it hard to say good-bye to a faithful friend.

References

1. Scott M. Cutlip and Allen H. Center. *Effective Public Relations.* 5th ed. Englewood Cliffs, N.J., Prentice-Hall, 1978, p. 111.

2. Rebel L. Robertson. "Public Relations for the Nonprofit Organization," in: Philip Lesly. *Lesly's Public Relations Handbook.* 2d ed. Englewood Cliffs, N.J., Prentice-Hall, 1978, p. 263.

3. Raymond A. Bauer. "The Audience," in: *Handbook of Communication*, ed. by Ithiel de Sola Pool and Wilbur Schramm, et al. Chicago, Rand McNally College Publishing Co., 1973, p. 145.

4. Contemporary use of this appeal has been researched and reported by Wilson Bryan Key in *Media Sexploitation* (New York, New American Library, 1976) and *Subliminal Seduction* (New York, New American Library, 1973). His work has been discredited (see Stephen Fox's *The Mirror Makers: A History of American Advertising and Its Creators.* Vintage, 1985, pp. 318–19) in recent years, but the basic message that sex sells appears to be still valid.

5. It must be kept in mind that T-shirt and button wearers do not always espouse the message they are sporting. They may

simply need something to wear, or find the sentiment expressed clever. It does not mean that the individual is necessarily a firm believer in the message.

6. David Ogilvy. *Confessions of an Advertising Man*. New York, Ballantine, 1963, p. 95.

7. Marshall McLuhan and Quentin Fiore. *The Medium Is the Message: An Inventory of Effects*. New York, Bantam, 1967, p. 26.

8. In fact, the introduction of mass media organizations as the relay for messages between the sender and the receiver is an additional communication factor (sometimes even a barrier), according to W. Phillips Davison and Frederick T. C. Yu, *Mass Communication Research: Major Issues and Directions*. New York: Praeger, 1974, pp. 6–7.

9. Vance Packard. *The Hidden Persuaders*. New York, Pocket Books, 1958, pp. 127–28.

10. Jurgen Ruesch. *Disturbed Communication*. New York, Norton, 1972, pp. 34–35.

11. Norman Turner. "Marketing the Library Service—Sales and Promotion," *European Journal of Marketing* 18 (1984): 72–81.

12. Jacquelyn Gavryck and Ruth Peabody. "Shaping the Library's In-House Publications Policy," *Wilson Library Bulletin* 54 (December 1979): 230–35.

13. Joan Ariel, ed. *Library Instruction Clearinghouses, 1985, A Directory*. Chicago, American Library Association/ Association of Research Libraries, 1985.

14. Martin Fox, ed. *The Print Casebooks: First Annual Edition: The Best in Annual Reports*. Washington, D.C., RC Publications, p. 5.

15. Association of Research Libraries, Office of Management Studies. *SPEC Kit #4: Internal Communication: Policies & Pro-*

cedures. Washington, D.C., The Association, May 1979, cover page.

16. Peter Wildbur. *International Trademark Design.* New York, Van Nostrand Reinhold, 1979.

17. David Acker and John Myers. *Advertising Management: Practical Perspectives.* Englewood Cliffs, N.J., Prentice-Hall, 1975, p. 430.

18. The NBC peacock was originally used to symbolize NBC's color capabilities. The peacock was retired when color television became commonplace. When the peacock returned in the late 1970s it was used to evoke the network's former days of glory (at that point it was trailing in the network rating battle) with the slogan, "NBC, proud as a peacock." The peacock is currently part of a new logo design.

19. Louis E. Boone and David L. Kurtz. *Contemporary Marketing.* 3d ed. Hinsdale, Ill., Dryden, 1980, p. 109.

20. David Ogilvy. *Confessions of an Advertising Man.* New York, Ballantine, 1963, p. 107.

21. Robert G. Neubauer. *Packaging: The Contemporary Media.* New York, Van Nostrand Reinhold, 1973, p. 57.

22. This is interesting in view of the fact that in sign shape language, those enclosed in circles are restrictive messages, such as "No Smoking."

23. Cosette Kies. *Problems in Library Public Relations.* New York, Bowker, 1974, pp. 107–09.

24. "Wooing's What They Do Best," *New York Times,* 2 March 1980, p. F17.

25. Jean Stafford. "Christmas Books for Children," *The New Yorker* (3 December 1973): 194–220.

26. Jane Anne Hannigan and Kay E. Vandergrift. "A Report of Research on Student Views," in: Jane Anne Hannigan and

Glenn Estes, eds. *Media Center Facilities Design*. Chicago, American Library Association, 1978, p. 22.

27. For example: Mona Garvey. *Library Displays, Their Purpose, Construction and Use*. New York, H. W. Wilson, 1976. And, Araminta Neal. "Display Techniques." (Slide/tape.) Nashville, American Association for State and Local History, n.d.

28. Stephen Delfin. "Alternatives to Donated Public Service Time," *Public Relations Journal* 40 (April 1984): 10–11.

29. Association of Public Service Directors. "Public Service Opportunities on Radio and Television," *Communication Forum* (February 1979): 1–2.

30. Mabel L. Conet. "History of the Friends of the Library," in: Sarah Wallace, ed. *Friends of the Library*. Chicago, American Library Association, 1962, pp. 2–3.

31. Ann Gwyn, Anne McArthur and Karen Furlow. "Friends of the Library," *College and Research Libraries* 36 (July 1975): 272–82.

32. Association of Research Libraries, Office of Management Studies. *SPEC Kit 6: Friends of the Library*. (April 1974, updated 1977.)

VIII ANALYSIS, EVALUATION AND MARKETING RESEARCH

THE IMPORTANCE OF identifying purpose, planning, and appropriate use of techniques cannot be overstated in carrying out public relations and marketing. Another critical area in the process, and probably the weakest one in actual practice, is evaluation for the purpose of continuous planning for the future. In spite of the attention libraries have paid in recent years to output measures, there is still a regrettable lack of precision in the evaluation of library PR and marketing. This is due not so much to a lack of interest and/or ability on the part of librarians, but rather to the nebulous nature of some elements within the PR/marketing process.

Measurement of Attitudes and Image

One problem appears to derive from the great desire to look at attitudes about the library and librarians, at the image of the institution and the profession. These elements are the least measurable of all, and this can often result in frustration for the librarian, who may sometimes retreat into defensiveness over any implied or blatant negative reference to libraries or librarians. This reaction may even result in a general hangup about evaluating PR and marketing at all, which is unfortunate, since there are some very useful measurements which can be applied. Although these measurements do not provide

133

neat, clear-cut evaluations of broad public opinion, they can provide clues about citizen and user feelings about the library, its collection, its services, and even the librarians.

The mainstay of attitude measurement is the survey. A number of different types of surveys have been used to measure public opinion about various aspects of libraries. Generally, they are defined in terms of the target groups and/or the manner in which the surveys are conducted.

During the past decade the growing use of A *Planning Process for Public Libraries*[1] in many communities has clarified three useful target groups on which librarians can focus in conducting surveys. The citizen survey samples opinions from an entire community. A second type of survey focuses on the library user group, which will obviously be the most knowledgeable about the library's current collection, services and programs. Finally, it is often useful to conduct surveys with a major user and potential user cluster, such as students. Because their needs are often more curricula-based, the data collected from student users will sometimes result in different opinions about the library.

In marketing circles it is more common to consider surveys in terms of the manner in which they are conducted. Specifically, surveys are often broken down into how the interviews to collect data are handled; such as interviews by mail, by telephone, or in person. A number of variations of these exist; for example, the increasing use of quick telephone interviews combined with immediate computer input in order to obtain fast results for public opinion polls.

All of these have obvious advantages and disadvantages. Mail surveys usually result in low percentage returns. Telephone interviews must to be kept short if the respondent is going to stick with the survey for the full period, and face-to-face personal interviews are expensive to conduct and often difficult to arrange, resulting in smaller samples and sometimes skewed results. Among the criteria to be considered before deciding upon which kind of survey to use are:

1/ Complexity of the survey.
2/ Required amount of data to be included in the survey.

3/ Desired accuracy, since quick telephone interviews conducted by volunteers may well result in a higher ratio of mistakes on a tally sheet.

4/ Sample control, or number of interviews needed to produce a statistically valid cross section.

5/ Time requirements, since stretching a survey over too long a period of time may produce invalidity on the basis of changing conditions.

6/ Acceptable level of response, or return.

7/ Cost, since surveys can be very expensive in terms of personnel. [2]

There are many things to consider in formulating survey questionnaires, identifying target groups and conducting the interviews. Most important is the basic reason for the survey and how the results will be used, for a survey is not the end product in itself.

Another consideration is the interview technique. Mail surveys, of course, are structured for easy response and are often set up so that the respondent merely needs to check off alternatives. Personal interviews, by telephone or on a one-to-one basis, may be devised either for structured responses or for open-ended replies. They can provide the benefit of eliciting comments not anticipated by the questionnaire designers, and may bring out some aspects about the library which had not been thought of earlier, but such results are more difficult to tabulate.

A variation on verbal questioning and response is use of a cartoon-type illustration with respondents being asked to fill in the blank balloon. An example of this technique is the patron and librarian cartoon shown in Figure 3. This was designed to help discover the attitudes of respondents about librarians. By asking them to quickly fill in the blank conversation balloon with the librarian's answer, the interviewer should find out something about respondents' expectations of librarians in general. Since the space is small, the written response will necessarily be short, and therefore easier to categorize. Interestingly enough, to date, only positive responses, such as "Sure, what do you want to know?" have been received,

WHAT IS THE LIBRARIAN

GOING TO SAY?

Fill in the response you think the librarian is going to say
to the library user. Then fill in the information below:

YOUR OCCUPATION _____

YOUR SEX _____   YOUR APPROXIMATE AGE _____

ARE YOU A REGULAR LIBRARY USER? _____

WHEN WAS THE LAST TIME YOU USED THE LIBRARY? _____

THANK YOU FOR YOUR HELP!

Figure 3
Fill-in-the-response Attitude Indicator

which leads this investigator to believe that public opinion about librarians is basically positive. A study involving teenagers, however, might produce different results, since some studies, including one conducted by Donald Gallo, showed that teenagers tend not to ask librarians for reading advice. The Gallo survey reveals that teenagers are greatly influenced by the librarians with whom they come in contact, so that a librarian who is unfriendly or strict is less likely to be approached for help or advice.[3] In such cases the cartoon librarian's response might well indicate a more negative image.

A by-product of a well-conducted survey is a general raising of consciousness about the library. In a citizen survey a number of people may find out about materials and services they had not known about previously. Users may consider additional library use, and students may end up thinking better of the library just because their opinions were asked. A difficulty some marketers find with surveys is people's irritation about taking time to answer questions for someone else's commercial gain. There is usually, however, goodwill on the part of the public in cooperating with a library survey, which in itself is indicative of the overall public attitude toward libraries.

Testing the Climate

In marketing much attention is paid to testing new products by means of panels and test markets. Because these techniques emphasize products, librarians have not used them as much as they have used surveys for evaluation. Some variations of these marketing measurement staples, however, have been used quite effectively by librarians in testing ideas for new services and programs.

Panels, often used in marketing for tasting (literally for food products and figuratively for preferences), are set up by the tester for the purpose of collecting quick data, or for a longer period of time to track changing attitudes and/or behavior. A third type of panel consists of a number of individuals who provide information only intermittently about specific products, items, or individuals. Long-term panel members are often asked to keep diaries, or logs, regarding certain choices. A sophisticated version of this technique is used by evaluators of television watching habits (such as Nielsen), electronic devices being attached to viewers' television sets to record the needed information. In such situations, where financial stakes are high, more sophisticated and costly measuring devices are easily justifiable.

Other panel techniques include the use of simple mail questionnaires to individuals who have agreed to report their preferences and behavior. With single-purpose panels the individual members are generally brought together (not a requirement for longer-term panels) to "taste" and discuss various items. Most commonly used with food and drink products, taste panels can also be used to gather reactions to new fashions, appliances, and other types of consumer goods. One example of this type of product testing was described by a reporter in terms of a community group fund raiser, in which women of a mother's club agreed to be paid to test a new detergent.[4]

Librarians, although they have used other names for the technique, have also engaged in panel testing, usually by informally using groups of prospective users as a sounding board for ideas about new services and programs. As librarians and users know, new ideas are not easily come by, so it's usually up to the librarians to come up with ideas of new programs to try in the library. In such cases it is wise to test the ideas on staff and potential users before proceeding too far.

Librarians have made heavier use of the marketing technique usually described as test marketing, although they have not always carried the process through as thoroughly as is common in commercial marketing. What librarians often call a pilot study or a project is essentially the same as test marketing. In commercial test marketing, whole cities are often selected as "typical" markets for a certain product, and early sales of a new product are accompanied by consumer interviews (often at point of purchase) and careful analysis of sales data. In libraries, it is more usual to try out a new service or program in limited locations (such as one branch) before launching it system-wide. Another variation is to invest in a limited number of items (such as toys and games, video tapes, or posters) for loan purposes to see whether the new service is popular before additional money is spent on creating a full-blown service. A more elaborate example of test marketing is to try a bookmobile stop or a temporary kiosk library in a location that looks promising for a new branch. Librarians usually don't engage in lengthy, structured interviews with users of the new service, or program, but they do collect comments from users and certainly examine use and attendance statistics. Final decisions on whether to go ahead with extended services are very often based on this type of evaluation.

Statistical Data in Libraries

Evaluation of library public relations and marketing is seldom quantifiable, except for such specifics as analysis of mass media coverage, public response to specific publicity, and attendance at various programs. Evaluation of attitudes and opinions about the library is, as we have already pointed out, difficult. Often evaluation must be tied to other library processes, and therefore cannot be considered "pure" library PR /marketing measurement. Nevertheless, since public relations and marketing activities are conducted for the entire library, its collection, services, and programs, these statistics should be considered in the analysis of a library's PR/marketing program.

According to A *Planning Process for Public Libraries*, there are nine areas in which librarians can gather information and statistics about the library:

1/ Income
2/ Source of funds
3/ Expenditures
4/ Circulation
5/ Volume and types of information services
6/ Extent of out-of-library services

7/ Network activity
8/ Registered borrowers
9/ Facilities. [5]

Gathering quantifiable statistics in these nine areas over a period of time enables librarians to track trends, and these can often be related to the library's public relations and/or marketing efforts during the same period. If those who are involved in evaluation agree that overall use and reaction to the library's collection, services, and programs are elements indicative of the library's degree of success, then the public relations and marketing activities of the library clearly should be related to these essential statistics. Much attention is being paid today to quantifying the evaluation of various library functions, no doubt a result of society's current stress on cost-effectiveness and financial accountability.

Such evaluative statistics are not collected as an end in themselves, but are used for planning future activities, services, and events, completing the cycle of effective management. Increases in use can be used as justification for increased budget requests. The inability to meet identified needs can be used as a factor in the preparation of grant proposals for outside funding. Decreases in use can be used as a rationale for service cutbacks or program discontinuance. Librarians have learned that there is nothing like statistical evidence to reinforce arguments when funding matters or changes are being discussed with outside individuals and authorities. Responsible and honest use of statistics is an effective communication and public relations technique.

Statistics can be used in simple trend analysis, or in variations such as before-and-after measurement. Such analysis is sometimes referred to as pre-testing and post-testing, showing use (and sometimes understanding) before and after something changes, such as education/training, publicity designed to heighten awareness of a service, or the introduction of simplified circulation procedures. Pre-testing is usually done with individuals or groups to see how well they understand or perform, as in their use of the card catalog. After a structured unit on how to use the card catalog, the same individuals or groups can be tested again, and the results are compared to measure the success of the training program. Such pre-testing and post-testing is more common in school and academic libraries, perhaps because statistical results are understood and valued in those environments, and also because of a desire to help educate library users. Formal pre-testing and post-testing is less frequently done in public and special libraries, since these environments are better suited to other forms of statistical gathering.

A telling example of how statistics can be used effectively is in the evaluation of public information campaigns. Consider some recent social-cause marketing campaigns, such as those on public littering and smoking. There is no question that changes have come about as a result of mass media publicity and public pressure. Statistics show that there is less littering and that some smokers quit. Media exposure has led to laws being changed, resulting in severe punishment for driving under the influence of alcohol and nonsmokers' areas in public places. When new laws and local ordinances occur as a result of changes in public opinion immediately following or during media campaigns, this is clear proof of success.

Internal Evaluation Techniques

Evaluation for libraries is done in various ways, sometimes employing publicity aimed at increasing public awareness and soliciting external assistance, and sometimes internally by the staff. In some cases, the evaluator might consider a combination of both external and internal processes, since the gathering information, including statistics and community data, must involve the public and the actual organization and analysis of the data are generally the responsibility of library staff.

One example of a survey which is closely related to the PR /marketing process is a communications audit. This audit tracks how people found out about certain events/ programs/information and their degree of satisfaction with the format, time, manner, and convenience of the message.[6] Such audits can produce effective quantitative measures because they focus on one aspect of the process, communication itself—which points up the need to keep data collection simple and focused. Although it is tempting to include and try to collect as much as possible when doing a survey, the results are almost always clearest when there is a single point that respondents understand.

Other models constructed for internal evaluation of public-relations activities generally include pertinent information about an activity, and focus evaluation on such factors as cost effectiveness or public response. A part of such evaluation activity is usually a recommendation for future action, such as continuing the PR activity, making changes, putting something else in its place, or stopping it altogether. Such models employ negative as well as positive results of the PR activity, and make for systematic evaluation.

Use of the Evaluation Results

Results of evaluation, whether derived from extensive citizen surveys or simple monthly circulation statistics, should be used as a basis for improving library performance and use. The public relations process uses evaluation results to explain changes, discuss trends, publicize activities, keep the public informed, plan for the future, and anticipate problems. Evaluation results are both news events and important tools for planning. By examining what libraries have done, librarians can more clearly see what needs to be done in the future. Effective positive change can only take place if one knows what has happened in the past, can quantify some aspects of that event, make a judgment as to its overall success or failure, and then plan on the basis of all this information. The future is shaped by examining the past.

References

1. Vernon E. Palmour, Marcia C. Bellassai and Nancy V. De Wath. A *Planning Process for Public Libraries*. Chicago, American Library Association, 1980.

2. Donald S. Tull and Del I. Hawkins. *Marketing Research: Measurement and Method.* 3d ed. New York, Macmillan, 1984, p. 126.

3. Donald R. Gallo. "Ask Your Librarian! Four Surveys Reveal Where Young People Turn for Reading Advice," *American Libraries* 16 (November 1985): 736–39.

4. "Testing Cereal in the Midwest," *New York Times*, 4 April 1982, p. F3.

5. Vernon E. Palmour, *et al., op. cit.*, p. 104.

6. Such a communication audit was designed by Cosette Kies and J. Michael Rothacker for school libraries and can be found in Cosette Kies, *Projecting a Positive Image through Public Relations.* Chicago, American Association of School Librarians–American Library Association, 1979, pp. 58–75.

7. Robert H. Ruffner. *Handbook of Publicity and Public Relations for the Nonprofit Organization.* Englewood Cliffs, N.J., Prentice-Hall, 1984, pp. 64–73.

IX DESIGNING A MARKETING/PR PLAN FOR A SPECIFIC LIBRARY

APPLICATION OF PUBLIC RELATIONS and/or marketing theory, principles, process, and techniques to a specific library is a step that involves considerable commitment and time. A number of decisions are needed before and during the planning process for implementation of a PR/marketing program. These decisions need to be made carefully and thoughtfully, for the success of the program could well depend on some of these initial judgments.

The first decision, clearly, is whether or not the library is going to commit itself to a planned PR and/or marketing program. All libraries use some public relations and marketing, but it is frequently not planned, and as a result the activities are often disorganized and the results erratic. In making the decision to plan a PR/marketing program, the library administration must decide on the person to head up the program, so that this person can be involved in the planning from the outset. Early consideration must also be given to budget. Even before individual activities are selected, a basic budget is necessary to maintain a reasonable level of ongoing publicity.

These initial decisions are generally made at top level, by the public library director and the library board, for example. Library directors with more autonomy may be able to make this kind of decision alone, or in consultation with the library staff. The staff should, in any case, be alerted to plans for any such major effort.

PR or Marketing?

Once the first commitment is made, other basic decisions must follow. Most critical at this stage is examination of the library's basic mission: it must either be reconfirmed or modified on the basis of top management thinking. Such a decision should emerge from such specifics as future budget and facility expectations, the existence of other libraries in the area, and the possibilities for networking with those libraries. Information about the community and the present condition of the library are other factors important in deciding whether to reaffirm or revise the library's *raison d'être*. In some library settings this decision is easy, for the library's basic mission was set down during its founding and has been updated along the way, as often applies in special, academic, and school libraries. Public libraries, however, must confront this issue squarely and make firm choices, for budgets seldom accommodate multi-philosophies and all-inclusive programs.

For public libraries this basic mission decision can mean a full commitment to community needs and desires, as in the much publicized decision by the Baltimore County Public Library to go for a library collection with attendant services and programs reflecting community use.[1] This decision was based on precisely the kind of community/library information that is needed in deliberations of this kind. The final decision was made to provide the citizens of Baltimore County with a library system that would complement other available libraries and center on the most frequent local demands of the community.

Such a decision is not the necessary outcome of a review of mission. It is entirely possible that another library might reconfirm and rededicate itself to its original purpose of building a balanced, quality book collection based more on librarians' judgments and evaluations than on community suggestions. The argument has been made in several places[2] that libraries should do just that, and adhere to the traditional values of librarianship. Another result of mission review might be to emphasize education or the provision of information.

In spite of the apparent "either/or" implications here, such decisions are not necessarily so dramatic and drastic. The library that has been conscientiously keeping pace with community needs and interests based on community analysis will already reflect a marketing philosophy based on those needs and interests. Commitment to local characteristics does not necessarily mean a desertion of the principles of book selection and collection development; a library can still work for quality collections within the framework of community need. The degree of balance in such collections may not be as high as in more traditional libraries after a period of time, but it will probably be adequate. The important thing is that the library has put community needs and interests first, and it is to the public's credit that in libraries such as BCPL this change in mission has not resulted in the entire book budget being spent on best sellers and genre fiction. [3]

A library may also choose to postpone a final decision on change and try the marketing approach in a few branch libraries before adopting the new philosophy system-wide. The Chicago Public Library has done this, and may eventually increase the number of locations where this philosophy is operative. Since CPL serves a research function as well, it would seem unlikely that the full library system would be committed to the marketing approach.

For those libraries not ready to go the full marketing way, the decision to have a planned program of public relations is still valid. A strong public relations program based upon two-way communication will strengthen that library's ties with the community and achieve much better rapport with it. A basic PR program does not exclude marketing, either; it is still possible to apply marketing techniques to some facets of library service and programming.

Planning

Once the decision is made to go ahead with either a marketing or a public relations program, someone needs to begin planning for the library. In some cases the library director will take on this responsibility, but in larger libraries a staff member is likely to be charged with this duty. That individual will gather information about the community and the library and consider how to build an effective program of communication.

It has been suggested that A *Planning Process for Public Libraries* is really a basic outline for building a marketing program,[4] and this is true. This planning process includes specific suggestions for community surveys and information gathering, plus advice on setting goals and objectives for the library. Clearly, a PR staff officer cannot undertake all of these tasks alone, and that first adminstrative decision on whether the library should undertake a public relations or a marketing approach is most important. Marketing requires continued top management involvement in the kind of activities outlined in the planning process document; the day-to-day operations of public relations can more easily be delegated to a staff member. In practice, the PR officer tends to use information about the community and the library that has already been generated elsewhere. The marketing director is more likely to initiate and carry out citizen surveys.

However it is gathered (and absorbed) by the PR officer or marketing director, this knowledge about the community is used as the basis for formulating a plan for the library's PR /marketing program. Individual goals and objectives should be set at this point, and activities considered which will accomplish the objectives. Budgetary limitations and the schedule will also come into play as the PR/marketing person designs a plan to achieve improved communication with the community and in the long run produce an improved image of the library.

The Publicity/Activity Calendar

A common and effective device for planning is a calendar which details activities for the library. Such a calendar will lay out the major elements of the program for a specific period (often such calendars are kept a year ahead), including such annual traditional events as a children's summer reading program in a public library, orientation tours and term paper clinics held by the reference staff every semester in an academic library, or a monthly breakfast in a special library for research staff. After scheduling the more permanent or regular events, the planner can then start to pinpoint one-time activities, focusing on special materials and programs, current events, television tie-ins, and current interests of people in the community. These calendars should be viewed as flexible, for unexpected opportunities can occur and should be taken advantage of, sometimes at the expense of other possibilities. For example, it would be foolish not to mount a display on a natural phenomenon such as an unexpected volcano eruption while public interest in the event is high. An originally planned display commemorating the anniversary of Elvis Presley's death could well be postponed to another time, perhaps even until the following year.

Careful planning of promotion activities is essential in order to avoid bunching events that might compete with each other, and to guard against dull periods with no activities. An activity/publicity calendar for a branch library might well include both activities generated for the entire system and special events celebrated only in the branch, such as an annual tea for neighborhood community leaders or programs of interest to neighborhood groups.

In addition to deciding on special focus events, it is important to plan with an eye to overcoming image problems and improving attitudes about the library. A community college library might well decide after a user survey that a special push needs to be made to encourage students and faculty to consult the library staff for assistance in selecting materials. This might result in a program devoted to a theme such as, "Need help? Ask your librarian." Focused programs of this sort may seem very simple and obvious, but they are a necessary part of PR /marketing plans. Very often, gaps in user perceptions will be uncovered in surveys, and the action necessary to alleviate the problem or misconception may be a very simple one. Another example is one encountered in public libraries, where it is often found that some nonusers don't use the library because they don't realize that its basic services and programs are free. What seems obvious is not always the image in the public's eye.

Techniques and Publicity

After basic planning is mapped out for a reasonable period of time, a strategy must be devised for publicity and promotion. Although a media blitz for all library activities may be desirable, it is not only economically unfeasible in most cases, but also may be unwise, since wholesale promotion can result in overwhelming some people to the point of boredom or even antagonism. Subtle reactions should be considered, because too much money spent on publicity, even if it is available, may cause people to wonder about the lavishness of such efforts, and this could lead to a reduced budget the following year. Common sense is an important part of public relations and marketing, and in this area especially it is critical.

In addition to generating such in-house publicity items as news releases, posters and other print materials, the PR /marketing planner needs to decide on outside sources. In some libraries the publicity pieces are done by freelance consultants and/or PR agencies. It may well be concluded that in the long run it is more cost effective for the library to contract with such outside experts, rather than invest in staff artists and printing equipment. In selecting a professional service, consideration should be given to:

/ Knowledge on the part of the source of conditions peculiar to the library.
2/ Experience in the specific type of project being considered.
3/ Competence in performing such a project.
4/ Reputation of the service in the community.
5/ Sensitivity to the special needs of the library.
6/ Ability to be flexible, if necessary.

Some libraries contract all publicity work to be done commercially, while other libraries do only occasional pieces outside. Such special instances might include a very nice printed item celebrating a special event, such as the opening of a new branch, which may be beyond the capabilities of the library's own production equipment. An example is Yeshiva University's graphically illustrating through a long photographic print the need for money for cataloging and shelving a gift collection of over 10,000 volumes. [5]

Another decision to be made, not as momentous perhaps, and one which can be easily changed, is whether or not to use library publicity materials available from such commercial publishers as the American Library Association, the Children's Book Council, and the like. Such decisions do not commit a library to a permanent course of action, and many libraries periodically decide on purchase of such materials based on the themes and artwork available at different times.

Deciding upon the variety of publicity materials available for each activity is one area in which the PR/marketing staff person spends much time, working with artists and photographers, and sometimes copywriters (if the PR/marketer is not doing the job personally), developing mailing lists, making media contacts and a variety of community contacts for distribution of publicity items. Staff members of the library should always be involved at this stage, for many of them belong to community groups and are able to distribute materials at meetings and/or make announcements about special programs and new services that the library is publicizing.

Appropriate agencies in the community need to be kept informed about special services and library programs, as do schools and the broader library community. If librarians are to cooperate and participate in networking activities, it only makes sense to inform their colleagues about what is going on in order to make them partners in publicity.

Evaluation

A variety of evaluation techniques exist to judge the effectiveness of PR/marketing programs (see chapter 8), but none of them evaluates the entire program, as is true with other organizational functions in libraries. The PR/marketing program is evaluated as are other programs within the library, examining personnel, output measures, and levels of service. By employing a variety of evaluation techniques it is possible to look at different elements within the PR/marketing program, diagnose weaknesses, and then make changes designed to strengthen the program.

The evaluative techniques generally used in assessing a specific library's PR/marketing plan consist of a combination of use/attendance statistics, and analysis of mass media and community comments. Such methods do not provide results as specifically quantifiable as one might like, but they do yield some feeling for the effectiveness of the program, and are an aid in diagnosing elements needing improvement. Commonly used statistics include circulation of materials on topics related to special displays and programs, or increased in-house use of materials such as career files, following special promotion efforts or public attendance at various meetings within the library. Outside the library it is also possible to gather statistics on the number of persons attending community groups at which the library is highlighted, or the number of individuals stopping at a special exhibit at a county fair or shopping mall.

Publicity campaigns can be measured by exposure in the mass media, the number of flyers distributed, and comments from library patrons and others in the community. Cost effectiveness should also be considered: were the costs of the publicity items justified by the public attention received?

In selecting the methods by which the PR/marketing plan's elements will be measured, an important factor is to facilitate the gathering of appropriate statistics over a period of time. These will make it possible to contrast before-and-after use, and to compare similar programs. Over a longer period it should be possible to spot trends, particularly important in helping to weed out programs that may be falling in popularity and interest.

In any evaluation one should always consider what might have been stressed more, what ideas might have worked better, and which items should be deemed failures. Such judgments enable the PR/marketer to plan better publicity for future activities, thus strengthening the program and, ultimately, the overall use of the library. Staff should be included in the evaluation process, particularly in the areas of weakness or failure, since they may be able to help identify reasons for the lack of success by providing library users' informal comments and reactions.

The decisions to be made about continuation of the PR/-marketing efforts may not seem as momentous as those required at the beginning of the process, but they are critical to the degree of success which the library can expect for its efforts in the future. Periodically, the library administration should review its whole program of public relations or marketing and consider anew what its primary focus should be in light of community needs. It is also essential to define again the library's main purpose, and whether or not the library should concentrate on marketing or public relations.

As with any program plan, each step along the way should be reevaluated, not only in regard to activities but in light of its place in the overall library and community picture. It is through continuous planning and evaluation that the library's PR/marketing program gathers strength in communicating the library's image to the wider community.

References

1. Ken Davis. "The Selling of the Library: Baltimore County System Challenges Library Role," *Publishers Weekly* 216 (13 August 1979): 26–28

2. Such as: Thomas H. Ballard. "More Books, Not Marketing Surveys," *American Libraries* 12 (February 1981): 76–78. And: John Berry. "Leaning toward Quality," *Library Journal* 104 (1 October 1979): 2013.

3. Nora Rawlinson. "Give 'Em What They Want!" *Library Journal* 106 (15 November 1981): 2188–90.

4. Peggy Barber. "A National Marketing Program for Libraries," *Illinois Libraries* 65 (March 1983): 188.

5. Harvey Shaman. "The Long Print," *Photomethods* (September 1984): 42–44, 55.

X LIBRARY MARKETING AND PR FOR NATIONAL EFFORTS

PUBLIC RELATIONS and marketing are used not only by the wide variety of individual libraries, but in multiple library situations as well. Regional library systems, state libraries, and state library associations have made good use of PR and marketing, as have some national institutions. Individual libraries can capitalize upon these national efforts by localizing them with specific information. If nothing else, national efforts have provided general publicity which is helpful in improving the overall library image with the public.

An examination of these current national efforts illustrates some important points in regard to PR and marketing for libraries, including the value of using the talents of top-rated designers and promoters to produce materials. There also is awareness of the value of using various publicity channels to enhance the library image, and the necessity for various forms of lobbying to increase chances for positive library legislation at local, state and national levels.

State Library PR Plans

A number of state libraries have seen the value of public relations in achieving their long-range goals for state library development. The Minnesota Office of Library Development and Services, Department of Education is one example. Included in its program is an overall goal:

155

> To achieve widespread and intensive public awareness of
> the many and varied library services and resources available to
> Minnesota citizens, concomitantly reducing the size of tradi-
> tional non-user groups, increasing the number of users, and
> expanding the use by current users. [1]

This basic goal is followed by a section drawing attention to
the Minnesota Governor's Pre-White House Conference and
the White House Conference on Library and Information Services itself, which recommended various resolutions regarding
library public relations. Four objectives with associated tasks
are then set forth:[2]

> 1/ To assist library personnel to understand the image they
> project to the users and non-users of their communities; to
> understand how to use public relations methods and tech-
> niques to improve the image of the library, personnel, ma-
> terials and services.
> 2/ To improve and increase the promotion of library services
> by means of all possible media.
> 3/ To encourage sharing of public information resources and
> expertise among all libraries.
> 4/ To ensure that library services are responsive to community
> interests and needs.[3]

Tasks associated with these objectives include such items as
charging the state library with providing PR workshops for library staffs, encouraging use of the national library logo, and
maintaining a clearinghouse of promotional materials produced by various libraries. Also included are activities which
encourage local libraries to coordinate their PR activities
through regional systems and to engage in community analysis
studies.[4]

Such an outline is clearly useful to local libraries, for it
explains exactly what role the state library will play in public
relations, and what the state library's expectations are of local
libraries. In addition, it provides a link between local libraries
and the national level, in a sense creating a giant promotional
network of libraries at local, regional, state and national levels.

WHCLIST

A good example of what librarians working together to promote libraries can achieve is the 1979 White House Conference on Library and Information Services (WHCLIS). Although instigated at the national level by the National Commission on Library and Information Services and the American Library Association, it could never have succeeded without the cooperation of many libraries at state and local levels. In most states preliminary meetings were held and conferences promoted to identify citizen delegates for the national conference, and to pinpoint concerns and issues that needed to be discussed at the national level.

As with many White House conferences, the benefits lay not so much in the resolutions themselves as in the actions at the state and local level following the White House conference. Another benefit was the identification of concerned citizens throughout the country who are willing to work for improved libraries. Also, the publicity gained from the state conferences and the national conference was another contribution toward building a stronger, positive image of libraries in the public eye.

The interest generated by the White House Conference has not been allowed to dwindle and die. A taskforce (WHCLIST) has been formed to maintain the interest of citizen members, and one useful activity of the group has been to compile an inventory of actions taken at state level on the various recommendations of the conference. It is felt that another conference must be held, and legislation has been introduced for a White House Conference for 1989.

Lobbying for Libraries

For several decades librarians have been aware of the need to lobby at various levels for positive library legislation. The American Library Association has long maintained a Washington office for the purpose of keeping legislators at the national level informed about library issues and concerns. Some state associations have paid staff who monitor state legislation, in addition to informing state legislators about proposed library legislation. Those state associations that do not have paid staff for this purpose generally have a committee, or network, of association members who perform this function on a volunteer basis.

The results of past library legislation, such as the Library Services and Construction Act, the Elementary and Secondary Education Act and the Higher Education Act, have been discussed in other publications. At the state level there has been much constructive legislation, such as that establishing and supporting statewide library systems. The need to promote positive library legislation with a target group of legislators and their staffs has been amply demonstrated, and librarians have generally done their part to aid in the passage of such legislation. This is a specialized type of library promotion but its benefits can be great, and failure can result in setbacks for library development. Librarians have discovered that some of their most persuasive PR skills must be employed to tell the library story to legislators and convince them of the value to their constituencies of voting for positive library legislation.

The American Library Association

As was noted in Chapter 2, there was early awareness of the value of having staff at the ALA headquarters to concentrate on national image building for libraries. Although PR staff was eventually provided, there were insufficient personnel to engage in massive publicity efforts for libraries, and little was done on the scale which early agitators like John Cotton Dana had hoped for until the National Book Committee started National Library Week activities in the 1950s. Focusing on April, the designated month for NLW, the staff of the National Book Committee encouraged articles in national periodicals touting the value of libraries. When the National Book Committee and NLW disbanded in 1974, National Library Week was taken over by the American Library Association, transferring to ALA a process which could be used to contribute toward an improved public image of libraries.

The Public Information Office of ALA has continued to produce posters, radio spots and other materials promoting libraries which may be purchased for use during National Library Week, or at any time throughout the year. Additional projects have been undertaken by this office, such as the mounting of a national marketing plan to promote telephone reference service in libraries. This focus was selected because the Gallup survey of libraries in 1978 revealed that the majority of individuals surveyed were unaware of such services in libraries.[5] Undertaken with the cooperation of the Chief Officers of State Library Agencies, the "Call Your Library" campaign consisted of publicity materials along with ideas for local activities. Johnny Carson used some questions and answers from libraries on the *Tonight Show*; national periodicals printed ads, as well.[6] Overall, the campaign was deemed a success, although some criticisms were received. Some librarians thought the materials stressed trivial questions.[7] In certain areas, the campaign was not used locally because some small libraries still do not have telephones, and hence have no telephone reference service.

Other activities of the PIO/ALA include the publishing of *Openers*, a small tabloid newspaper about good reading, for quantity distribution in local libraries, and the continued promotion of the national library symbol.

The Center for the Book

Another national activity for promotion of books, reading and libraries, is the Center for the Book of the Library of Congress. Founded in 1977 under Public Law 95-129, the Center has in some ways compensated for the void left by the old National Book Committee, although with different projects and under different governance. Both the NBC and the Center for the

Book adopted the promotion of books and reading as a primary purpose.

Activities of the Center fall into a number of categories. In its national campaign to promote books and reading to the general public, the Center has provided "Read More About It" television spots to be used following selected CBS television specials. These spots suggest that viewers of the preceding program go to their libraries and bookstores to get books about the topic featured on the program. Some of the celebrities who have been featured in these spots include Nancy Reagan, Richard Thomas, Mikhail Baryshnikov and Mickey Mouse.[8]

The Center has also used a cartoon character, Cap'n O. G. Readmore, created by ABC-TV, in children's programming on television to promote family reading.[9] Yet another project was the "Books Make a Difference" series of interviews and a resulting book published by The Shoe String Press. In interviews conducted by Gordon and Patricia Sabine, hundreds of people were asked two questions: "What book made the greatest difference in your life?" and "What was that difference?"[10]

Another group the Center has targeted for activities is the professional audience. Projects for this group have included a number of symposia and publications dealing with books and reading.[11] An associated target group is scholars, and the Center has sponsored lectures, symposia, and traditional bibliographic studies and other publications for them.[12]

The Center for the Book is encouraging the growth of regional centers in order to promote books and reading at the state level. Florida inaugurated its Center in 1985, to be followed by Illinois, Minnesota, and other states.

Postage Stamps

One simple device for promoting libraries and reading is commemorative U.S. postage stamps. Since 1982, three such stamps have been produced (see Figure 4). One features the Jefferson Building of the Library of Congress. The second, brought about through the efforts of the American Library

Figure 4
U.S. Postage Stamps Commemorating Libraries and Reading

Association, features a graphic alphabet motif and the legend, "America's Libraries; Legacies to Mankind." The third, which promotes reading, was inspired by the Center for the Book and is based on a Brady photograph of Lincoln reading to his son; shown is the Center's slogan, "A Nation of Readers." All three stamps were designed by Bradbury Thompson.

Although it may seem a rather simple promotion technique, the highlighting of libraries and reading on postage stamps is effective, since many people collect stamps and most individuals at least glance at attractive stamps. A related technique is that of using library and book-related slogans on postage meters. Those libraries that are large enough to have their own postal meters can easily have special slugs made for their machines which will draw attention to libraries.

Literacy and the Ad Council

A recent project of the American Library Association and other organizations, united in the Literacy Coalition, has attracted the attention of the Advertising Council, which has made literacy one of its advertising themes. The Council produces high quality ads for print and electronic media, using the talents of its members. The ads are placed in the mass media. All this is provided as a public service by the Advertising Council, and has resulted in heightened public interest in the problem of functional illiteracy among adults in this country. Such assistance is far beyond what the Literacy Coalition, or its members, including ALA, could do. It is a strong argument for the idea that if a cause is worthy, there is no need to feel that working for it must be a lonely, solitary battle.

Publishers and Book Promotion

Libraries have long benefited indirectly from the advertising and promotion efforts of publishers, particularly those who issue trade books. Any promotion of the materials carried by libraries is beneficial for such promotion helps to stimulate public demand for these materials. Much of the publishers' promotion, of course, is designed to increase sales, but the result often is a demand from the public for specific titles in libraries. Some librarians tend to view such demand as something less than a benefit; meeting the demand for bestsellers, for example, has long been a problem for public libraries. Nevertheless, the fact that some part of the public views libraries as the place to go for books shows that this publicity is basically helpful to the institution.

Book-reviewing publications read by the public are also helpful to libraries in this way, since attention is often directed to titles of literary and/or scholarly merit, and a demand is created for the quality books that many librarians prefer to buy. Authors on television and radio talk shows are obviously promoting their own books, but such appearances also serve to promote the library's materials.

Some publishers' promotions are aimed directly at librarians as a target group of potential purchasers of books and other materials. Publishers' catalogs are the primary tool for this purpose, but other promotional devices are employed as well, including giveaways at librarians' conferences. In some cases, there have been full-fledged marketing approaches, designed to help librarians promote certain publications to the public. A notable example of this has been the Federal Depository Library Program's marketing campaign to encourage use of government documents in libraries. The campaign kit includes a specially designed logo, posters, promotional flyers and media releases and PSAs. Such materials have been very useful for librarians.

Cooperative Programs

Libraries are sometimes encouraged to cooperate with other national promotional ventures, such as National Hobby Month. Individual libraries that choose to cooperate with such programs often find that there are ready-made, generally attractive and usually free materials available for the library's use. As with other national programs, libraries have the opportunity to associate with ongoing publicity centered on something besides libraries per se, with the additional advantage of obtaining some positive publicity with minimum effort.

Coalitions

Originally thought of in terms of a political strategy, coalitions enable librarians to join with others in projects of value to more than one group and to benefit from the public relations efforts that such coalitions can provide. Generally, coalitions are thought of as being not only political in nature, but cause-oriented. In such cases as the Literacy Coalition, where the cause is one that librarians can identify as being related in some way to libraries, attaching the library's name to the cause is not likely to be controversial. A noncontroversial coalition founded in recent years by ALA is that involving a number of national organizations in the support of National Library Week. In other situations, such as those related to social issues, some librarians have trouble in justifying the library's involvement. Such social causes have created controversy within ALA regardless of the "right of the cause," because some members feel that libraries and librarians should not support one side or another because of the library's duty to present all sides of an issue. Such a cause in recent time has been the growing issue of human rights in South Africa, one result of which has been that some institutions and associations, including ALA and some universities and libraries, have disposed of stocks of companies doing business with the white government of that country. Some librarians believe there is a moral right involved, and that librarians and their institutions should make plain the concerns of individuals and groups in such cases.

Less intense in nature are coalitions that work for the public good, including not only the before-mentioned cause of literacy, but the provision of aid to unemployed individuals to find work, assistance in providing meaningful after-school activities for latchkey children, and other projects directed at improving the community as a whole. By involvement in such activities and coalitions, librarians as individuals and libraries as institutions engender good will and enhance the reputation of the agency, ultimately contributing to a better image of the library.

References

1. Minnesota Department of Education, Office of Library Development and Services. "Minnesota Long-Range Plan for Library Service 1985," *Minnesota Libraries* 27 (Autumn 1984): 320.

2. *Ibid.*

3. *Ibid.*

4. *Ibid.*, pp. 320–21.

5. The Gallup Organization, Inc. *Book Reading and Library Usage: A Study of Habits and Perceptions, Conducted for the American Library Association*, Princeton, N.J., The Gallup Organization, 1978, p. 22.

6. Peggy Barber. "A National Marketing Program for Libraries," *Illinois Libraries* 65 (March 1983): 187–90.

7. *Ibid.*

8. Robert A. Carter. "The Center for the Book: Seeking Outreach," *Publishers Weekly* 227 (4 January 1985): 30–34.

9. John Y. Cole. "Reading and Book Promotion, Recent Center for the Book Activities," *LC Information Bulletin* 42 (16 May 1983): 160.

10. John Y. Cole. "Oral History and the Printed Word, A Report on Recent Center for the Book Activities," *LC Information Bulletin* 40 (19 June 1981): 218.

11. Robert A. Carter, *op. cit.*, p. 31.

12. *Ibid.*, pp. 31–32.

XI CURRENT TRENDS IN LIBRARY MARKETING AND PR

SOME OF THE NEWER FORMS of public relations and marketing a e not so much new in themselves as older forms given a new emphasis and clearer purpose. Changed emphases bring out objectives more clearly, and demonstrate the need to evaluate appropriately and truthfully. In tracing the development of public relations and marketing in libraries, the evolution of these fields into important parts of library management and function can be seen. The current scene in library PR and marketing illustrates the continued effort to clarify and improve the library's image, basic purpose, and scope of activities.

The Image

The image of the library held by the public has long been a concern of librarians. A related concern, and at times apparently one of higher priority, seems to be the image of librarians themselves in terms of basic appearance and personality, not to mention status and salary. This personal concern is not new; articles and comments in the library literature have dealt with this topic since the beginning of the modern profession.[1] Although this personal concern may sometimes seem trivial, the image of librarians certainly plays a part in the overall image of the library. Although librarians complain about how they are viewed in the public eye,[2] these complaints do bring out certain derogatory features, such as appearance (old maidish) and character traits (shy and given to detail). On the other hand, librarians do not always recognize that they are actually held up as believable people by the advertising business. Professionals do not like the ads which show libraries and librarians as quiet and stodgy but they tend to overlook the implied compliment in some of those ads which show librarians as "knowing what they are talking about."[3] One can only hope that this positive part of the image is retained in the overall impression people have about libraries. After all, if librarians are viewed as believable people, then it should follow that libraries are institutions that provide believable information. The concern with image is an important consideration. In order to attract people and make them firm supporters, if not regular users, the library has to be seen in a favorable light.

The problem seems to lie not with how to project an image of the library, but in reaching agreement on exactly what image it is that the profession wants to send forth. Herein lies one of the perpetual paradoxes of library promotion: since librarians cannot agree as a profession on what libraries are (primarily because of different opinions about the purposes of various libraries), they cannot send out a clear message. Even within types of libraries there is no solid agreement, for a community-college learning center often projects a different image of its collection and services than does a large university library. These differences can be seen easily at the local level where there is usually more than one library, and the differences are compounded at the state, national, and international levels. No wonder that librarians have problems in translating some of their most basic purposes into clear and simple messages for the public. If the profession cannot settle on a coherent image, public confusion is to be expected.

Merchandising

This basic problem with image carries over into some of the newer trends in libraries, such as merchandising library collections and services. Merchandising is generally thought of in connection with display and sales relationships, but in a library it can be viewed as a form of promotion. Specifically, it is a way to demonstrate visually and through personal behavior that the library is eager for people to find its wares attractive. Library collections and services are meant to be used, not puzzled over and/or ignored. An aggressive posture which says "Use me!" provides an obvious parallel with commercial establishments where the message "Buy me!" is a primary motive.

One library that has adopted merchandising is the Public Library of Anne Arundel County in Maryland. The primary purpose was to increase circulation of library materials. The three ways in which this could be accomplished, according to the authors of a display manual for the library, are:

1/ By prominently featuring high demand stock in heavy patron traffic areas.

2/ By stimulating patrons to borrow materials about subjects or themes with which they might not otherwise have had contact.

3/By arousing patron impulse in such a way as to cause them to borrow one or more additional items than they had intended when they entered the library.[4]

Merchandising library materials within the library means displaying resources in a manner that has proven to be successful in commercial establishments. These include: up-front displays, end-of-aisle displays, cross-aisle displays, pryamid displays, paperback dumps, face-out display of books, eye-level displays, point-of-purchase displays, open floor displays, displays at angles to patron traffic, zig-zag shelving, and pyramid/step displays.[5]

Other principles of merchandising include keeping displays ever-changing, fresh-looking, and attractive. Merchandising should encourage library users to pick up materials just as they pick up items in a grocery store when waiting for check-out. The same psychology is at work, that of enticing users (buyers) to select something beyond what they originally set out to find.

Merchandising is another step forward in promoting libraries. In the past there was debate over whether or not it was appropriate for libraries to be publicized at all. Now some librarians have committed themselves not only to the principles of promotion but to merchandising within the library. It is not considered enough to get people to come to the building. Now more use of the materials within the library is to be encouraged by knowledgeable display of resources. This is a logical progression, for promotion describing the library usually features enthusiastic descriptions of what is available there. It follows that this fact should quickly be made evident to the users entering the library. To quote Fred Glazer's argument:

> Today's fund-seeking librarian would do well to be a cross between P. T. Barnum and Muhammad Ali. A more aggressive philosophy of librarianship is needed, from keeper of books to seller of services. One that is patterned after the great merchandisers. After all, we're competing with all agencies of government for our share of the funding.[6]

Selling Information

Some librarians believe that libraries should be promoted as information providers, rather than suppliers of more traditional library services. The rationale is that in today's world information is the key element for survival, and that by stressing information functions libraries will make themselves indispensable.

This emphasis, however, is no more a panacea for libraries than a focus on traditional collections, services, and programs, because information services are no more unique to libraries than the traditional elements. Information can be obtained in many places other than the library, just as many of the traditional materials and services can be found elsewhere. It is, then, no easier to project a firm, simple image of a library based purely on information provision than it is to project a clearly undertsood image of the more traditional library. The answer does not seem to lie in a shift of the focus of the library's basic purpose.

There is agreement, nevertheless, that in projecting the library's image a strong factor is the role of the agency as a place to get information that has been collected, manipulated, organized and retrieved through modern technology. Libraries have long been involved in the information explosion; they need to emphasize this in promotion, so that members of the public understand that when they want information, the library is the place to get current and unbiased answers. It should be understood, though, by librarians and users alike, that although librarians are using new technologies, they have not excluded books and traditional services as outdated.

Some information specialists have suggested that information as a need may have been overemphasized. "Customers with the 'need-to-know,' such as librarians and financial analysts, defined their jobs around information products. Not today."[7] This author goes on to say, "The new markets for growth are populated by a different breed of customer with a cool 'nice-to-know' attitude."[8] Substance should be stressed, along with reliability. Some information is essential, that is true, but not all information is vital. By recognizing degrees of need, librarians and information specialists can better understand the information function of the library and the role it plays in the delivery of library services.

For those agencies, such as special libraries, where information has been and remains the dominant function of the enterprise, the marketing of information is paramount. The basic steps to consider are really no different from the marketing principles already discussed. They are to:

1/ Uncover the need.
2/ Emphasize the benefit.
3/ Differentiate your product.
4/ Find a niche.
5/ Explore alternative distribution channels.[9]

Although these points were designed to apply to selling a specific commercial information service, there is clearly an application for libraries. Certainly, if libraries intend to provide users with what they need, it is necessary to identify their information needs and let them know that the library can help. If information is the primary need of the library's users, then information is what the library should provide. Special libraries in particular must be client-centered, or they will quickly become obsolete.

While information is not necessarily the basic ingredient of all library functions and promotions, it may be essential for some. Information, while the basic commodity for some libraries, cannot be used as the lone support for the image of libraries in general.

CATV

The potential of cable television (CATV) became evident to libraries in the early 1970s, and great interest ensued in the possibilities of using cable to carry library services, programs' and promotion into the home. A few libraries, such as the public library in Casper, Wyoming, started using cable television a number of years ago in a variety of ways, including story-hour presentations for children and telephone/television reference service.

To date, the full potential of cable television as a library service has not really materialized, although an increasing number of libraries have received licenses to run public-service channels in their viewing areas. The principal reason for the lack of development in this field may have been lack of available money, since this type of service is expensive to operate and requires the special expertise of television technicians and programmers. In some ways, the use of cable television seems to have paralleled the development of radio use by libraries. In past decades, some libraries had library programs on community radio stations, often book talks, chat shows about new books, interesting reference questions, and interviews with visiting authors. A very few even ran their own radio stations, such as those in Louisville, Kentucky, and Nashville, Tennessee. The latter's station has been pushed into foundation-supported status in recent years. The costs, both in dollars and in personnel time, has restricted the participation of most libraries in radio to little more than promotion through public service announcements.

Cable television is being used to some extent, particularly in some rural areas where the servicing/programming aspects of the medium constitute a real boon to the community. The public library serving Atlanta and Fulton County, Georgia, maintains a TV studio and a regular schedule of programs on cable. The expense remains a factor, but it can be justified better in some communities than others. The promise of CATV for libraries has not yet been fulfilled but interest in its potential remains, and some libraries may yet be able to develop strong television services and programs.

External Fund Raising

Libraries are no strangers to gifts and endowments. Indeed, many libraries owe their beginnings to magnificent gifts from the wealthy during the age of philanthropy, and many still bear the names of their original benefactors. Through the years gifts have continued to come to libraries; sometimes they have been solicited and sometimes they have come as happy surprises. Some great libraries, including some important research facilities, have been largely or totally dependent on funding from private sources.

Many libraries have been the recipients of smaller gifts, such as memorial gift books honoring deceased relatives and friends, and a number have received bequests in wills, some large enough to start collections. Various community groups have made gifts to libraries through the years, some of them regular or earmarked for specific projects, such as the acquisition of large-print books, and others more occasional in nature. Even gifts of books which are inappropriate for the library's collection can contribute to the library by means of resale at book fairs. Occasional large gifts have come from corporations and businesses that desire to make a contribution to the quality of life of the community. Today, however, there is less reliance on happy surprises, and librarians have moved into an aggressive search for supplementary funding.

With budget restrictions growing higher more and more libraries, even those formerly supported totally by means of public money, have begun to look to sources of private funding. This search for additional money is often considered an essential element in a library's PR program, for it involves especially delicate communication and promotion.

Planning will achieve more than mere hope in this process, and many libraries have begun to formulate a planned strategy for external funding. Since many public-supported universities have long been engaged in seeking private funds as well as special or governmental grants, university libraries have become quite experienced in this area. The major focus in the past has been on governmental grants,[10] interest in private foundations as a source of funding is increasing rapidly.

Experience in applying for grants has taught librarians the desirability of focusing proposals on specific purposes, either ones already spelled out in the original allocation of funds, or to relate library development to the areas emphasized by foundations. Librarians have found that money does not flow easily into library coffers without extraordinary effort on their part. Association with a reputable institution such as libraries is no longer a sufficient attraction for many donors: it is necessary for staff to move into aggressive fund seeking.

Success in seeking money aggressively requires a planned approach. Haphazard approaches usually produce haphazard results, and the necessity of a plan, or strategy, has become more and more evident to librarians studying ways to obtain additional money. There have been amazingly successful results in some locations, as evidence by the recent renaissance of the New York Public Library—the product of an active, informed financial plan to attract private money to the library.[11]

Library Foundations

An early strategy adopted by libraries in the search for outside money was the formation of a Friends of the Library group.

Since Friends groups could be easily set up as separate tax-exempt associations, they could raise money for the library, accept gifts on behalf of the agency and then pass them on to the library without legal difficulties. Some libraries, notably the strong research libraries established with private money, set up endowments, the income from which provided basic operating funds, and also sought additional money for special acquisitions and projects.

In recent years, another funding mechanism that has become more popular is the library foundation. Examples, not limited to research libraries, include the California State Library Foundation,[12] the Wisconsin Library Association,[13] and a number of academic and public libraries. Some of the advantages for a library in setting up a foundation are summarized by Suzanne Landrum, Director of Marketing for the Denver Public Library: "a foundation is a tool to handle private money."[14] It protects private money from being swallowed up in a general budget derived largely from public money, and leaves options to handle gift money as the library sees fit, within the stipulations of the gift itself. A library foundation is not set up to provide money to other grant seekers but to serve as a conduit for outside funds designed to benefit the library. For that reason, it fits the definition of a community foundation, which is "characterized by multiple sources of funding, and a local or regional focus in . . . giving."[15]

Among libraries which have found this method to be very positive are the Broward County, Florida, Public Library and the Tulsa, Oklahoma, City-County Library. Certain principles have been found effective by these and other libraries in seeking funds through library foundations. One is the principle of cause-related marketing; another is the importance of establishing a funding strategy; and finally there is the need to target potential donors, to suggest specific amounts of donations to them, and to personalize approaches whenever possible.

Cause-related marketing is a technique by which business interests can be served by helping an institution such as a library. It serves the mutual benefit of both the donor and the donee. In Broward County, a specific campaign was engaged in by the library and American Express, enabling that company to advertise its help while providing added promotion to the library. All this advertising of this sort was totally free to the library and beyond the actual monetary gift given to the library by the Company. A fund-raiser dinner, underwritten by the Company, provided the library with yet more money and added publicity from coverage of the event itself. By promoting the library, American Express was able to promote itself and gain stature in the area as a supporter of a respected community organization which had sold itself to the Company as a responsible and important agency. One of the tactics used by the library to represent itself to American Express was to class itself with United Way agencies, providing a handle of sorts for the Company to visualize the library as being worthwhile.[16] In essence, the library positioned itself in the potential donor's mind as comparable to other agencies with which it was more familiar than with the library.

Funding strategies vary among library foundations, but in all cases the foundation needs to understand clearly how the funding will be used by the library receiving it. Local funding should be clearly separated from state and federal funding, and private funds designated even more clearly.[17] How the money is spent is critical, since funds will probably have been solicited for specific purposes. If money is being sought for an endowment fund, this should be made plain to the potential donor; this is equally true of small amounts solicited for specific purchases for the library. One library foundation in Janesville, Wisconsin, has hit upon the idea of a gift catalog for potential donors, describing various items and services which may be obtained by the library for specific donor dollars.[18]

The importance of personalizing appeals to potential donors was thought through by foundation staff in Tulsa. A series of VIP breakfasts was held throughout a year-long campaign to build an endowment fund for the library. Personal visits to potential donors, after research on each donor's background, plus much persistence, paid off. Each corporation was targeted for a specific amount of money, and some provided even more then was targeted.[19]

A final touch to the campaign in Tulsa was a year-long

celebration for everyone in the community to highlight the library's twentieth anniversary. Built around the theme, "Happy birthday, library, and many happy returns!", many activities were planned to include everyone who wanted to be involved, and to counteract the long-range potential problem that people might begin to see the library as an elitist institution, geared to the interests only of the rich.[20]

Current Issues and Trends

As can be seen from these examples, the current scene in library public relations and marketing involves interest in strategies, stress, and attitudes. An added interest is in doing things the right way, learning how to do things successfully from the experts. There seems to be a greater acceptance of going outside the narrow confines of librarianship to seek out successful tactics and schemes to help promote libraries, and also to rely more on outside experts. There is a growing realization that librarians may not be able to do everything themselves. Overall, there is a sense of growth and maturity in library public relations and marketing today.

References

1. Such as: Rosalie McReynolds. "A Heritage Dismissed," *Library Journal* 110 (1 November 1985): 25–31.

2. *American Libraries*, the official publication of the American Library Association, has a regular short column devoted to the image.

3. A representative of an advertising agent apologized to a nutrition scientist for using a librarian rather than a dietician in a proposed ad for bread, and explained that marketers had determined that librarians are viewed by the public as more believable than dieticians.

4. Que Bronson and Holly Stone. *Materials Display Manual.* Annapolis, Md., Anne Arundel County Public Library, 1981, p. 4.

5. *Ibid.*

6. Frederick Glazer. "Selling the Library," *Library Journal* 99 (1 June 1974): 1518.

7. Samuel H. Solomon. "What To Do When the Phone Stops Ringing," *Information Times* (Fall 1985): 12.

8. *Ibid.*

9. Sunday Lewis. "5 Lessons to Learn from the Software Industry," *Information Times* (Fall 1985): 16.

10. Association of Research Libraries, Office of Management Studies. *SPEC Kit 48: External Fund Raising in ARL Libraries.* Washington, D.C., The Association, May 1983, p. i.

11. Carl Bakal. "The Quiet Crisis: Are We Losing Our Libraries?" *Town and Country* (March 1983): 166–68, 251–58.

12. "California State Library Incorporates a Foundation," *Library Journal* 107 (15 June 1982): 1171.

13. John Bradbury. "Introduction," American Library Association, Library Administration and Management Association, Fund Raising and Financial Development Section Program Meeting, 7 July 1985.

14. Suzanne Landrum. "Will There Be a Library for Your Future?" American Library Association, Library Administration and Management Association, Fund Raising and Financial Development Section Program Meeting, 7 July 1985.

15. David F. Freeman. *The Handbook on Private Foundations.* Cabin John, Md., Seven Locks Press, 1981, p. 7.

16. Barbara Cooper. "The Foundation in Partnership with Business," American Library Association, Library Administration

and Management Association, Fund Raising and Financial Development Section Program Meeting, 7 July 1985.

17. Suzanne Landrum, *op. cit.*

18. *The Janesville Public Library Foundation Gift Catalog.* Janesville, Wis., The Foundation, 1985.

19. Pat Woodrum. "Endowment Fund Raising," American Library Association, Library Administration and Management Association, Fund Raising and Financial Development Section Program Meeting, 7 July 1985.

20. *Ibid.*

XII PUBLIC RELATIONS OR MARKETING: WHICH IS BEST FOR LIBRARIES?

PUBLIC RELATIONS AND MARKETING can be ignored by libraries, but only at their peril. The more common pattern that prevails is sporatic publicity, news releases issued from time to time when some special event occurs. Responsive libraries will recognize public relations and marketing as a process and build it into every operation from policy making to book shelving. Once at this point, the choice must be made between marketing in its full sense, including public relations, or public relations alone without the attention to promotion of use that marketing involves.

Throughout this book stress has been placed upon the process and program of public relations and marketing. This does not mean that it is purely a system, for its very success depends upon individuals—not only those who plan and execute the PR and marketing programs, but every person in the library organization. All staff members are part of the library's overall public relations/marketing process, and need to be involved in planning, implementing, maintaining, and evaluating the various PR/marketing systems. Each staff member who comes in contact with the public is a representative of the library and is a part of the library's image in the public's eye. Just as great damage can result from a circulation clerk's surly manner as from a poorly written news release. As a public service institution, the library must always be mindful of the importance of its many public contacts.

PR or Marketing?

Whether or not the library chooses to stress public relations or marketing in its organizational philosophy is not terribly important. Both systems are valid, and since the complete marketing process incorporates public relations, it isn't even necessary in some instances to make the choice. Even those libraries that elect to stay with the more familiar process of public relations as the basic image-building program for the library have made a good decision, for the philosophy and techniques of public relations are sound and helpful. Whichever the library chooses, PR or marketing, the important hurdle has been overcome. That hurdle is whatever resistance library management has had to "buying into" either system at all. Sporadic stabs at PR or marketing are not sufficient in today's volatile world. Only by instigating and maintaining a carefully designed program of PR or marketing can today's library succeed in building a positive and useful image in the public's eye. Positive public opinion about the library is essential for the library's survival, and librarians need to present and nurture a truthful, dynamic portrait of their institution. No one else is better equipped to do this than librarians and library advocates. Librarians must be the shapers of the library's image, as well as of its purpose. Libraries will survive to continue their role in society only if they are convincing in their image projection.

By projecting a positive library image librarians perform an important part of their basic job. As librarians, they are convinced of the value of libraries, but they cannot continue to assume that this value—is recognized or understood by the public at large. Only by making the strongest possible case for libraries can the purpose and value of this venerable agency be conveyed to the public. Librarians must be the ones to do the job. No one else is going to do it for them.

APPENDIX

RESULTS OF THE SURVEY TAKEN OF THE
PUBLIC RELATIONS SECTION OF THE
LIBRARY ADMINISTRATION AND
MANAGEMENT ASSOCIATION OF THE
AMERICAN LIBRARY ASSOCIATION, 1980

A SURVEY was taken of the membership of the Public Relations Section, Library Administration and Management Association, American Library Association in 1980. This group was used for the survey since its members could be considered: 1/ obviously interested and perhaps more knowledgeable than others about library PR, 2/ a representative geographic spread, 3/ representative of a number of types of libraries and library practitioners (with the majority being public libraries), and 4/ a controllable number of people for such a study.

Mailing labels of the membership of the PR Section were obtained from ALA. Some labels were pulled, specifically those of obvious library educators and/or students. The questionnaire itself also requested that only library practitioners respond. In all, 1,405 questionnaires were sent. The returned questionnaires were tabulated and analyzed by cross-tabulation manipulation. Some of the results have been referred to in the main body of this book, but the complete results of the survey are presented in this appendix.

Of the 1,405 questionnaires sent, 385 were returned. Since one was completed by a library educator, it was invalidated and 384 questionnaires were tabulated. Although the questionnaire was anonymous, a tally was kept of the postmarks as the questionnaires were returned, so it was possible to have a rough geographic accounting of the responses. The results showing this geographic spread follow:

Total number of questionnaires sent	1,405
Total number of responses	385
Number invalidated	1
Total number of responses tallied	384
Percentage of return	27

Number returned from the Northeast region	32
Number returned from the Mid-Atlantic region	41
Number returned from the Southeast region	60
Number returned from the Southwest region	32
Number returned from the North Central region	136
Number returned from the Mountain-Plains region	22
Number returned from the Pacific Northwest region	49
Illegible postmarks	9

Highest state responses:

Illinois	45
California	32
Michigan	24

States with no responses (unless postmark was illegible): Arizona; Wyoming; Idaho; Alaska; South Dakota.

None received from Canada or other foreign countries.

Following is a report of the responses. Immediately following each question is the number of usable replies in brackets. The answers, also shown in brackets, are reported as percentages of the total number of usable responses for each particular question. Percentages were rounded off, so amounts do not always add up to 100 per cent. Also, questions asking for a multiple response resulted in irregular totals, as did those which received only partial answers.

The introductory statement was:

As a member of the Public Relations (PR) Section of the Library Administration and Management Association (LAMA) of the American Library Association (ALA), I am asking your help in trying to determine the current state of library public relations as well as some attitudes about some aspects of library PR. The following questionnaire will take time to fill in, but your responses and return of the questionnaire will be very helpful to me in ascertaining various facts and opinions about library PR. I plan to use the information as part of a chapter in a book I am writing on library public relations. Your filling in and returning of the anonymous questionnaire in the enclosed, self-addressed envelope will be of great help to me and others who are interested in gathering and analyzing information in this area. I am very grateful for your help.

1. How long have you been a member of the PR Sections? (Please check below.) ⟨N = 380⟩
⟨25.3%⟩ Less than one year
⟨51.6%⟩ Between one and five years
⟨18.0%⟩ Between six and fifteen years
 ⟨4.2.%⟩ Over fifteen years

2. Check below the best description of yourself: ⟨N = 384⟩
⟨71.6%⟩ Primarily a general library administrator
 ⟨6.3%⟩ A library administrator spending at least ⅓ time on library PR
 ⟨5.5%⟩ A full-time library PR specialist employed by a library/libraries/system
 ⟨0.5%⟩ A full-time free-lance (self-employed) PR specialist
 ⟨2.3%⟩ A part-time library PR specialist employed by a library/libraries/system
 ⟨0.3%⟩ A part-time library free-lance PR specialist
 ⟨3.4%⟩ A librarian working primarily in non-administration and non-PR
 ⟨6.5%⟩ A branch or department head
 ⟨0.0%⟩ A volunteer library PR specialist
 ⟨0.0%⟩ A public library trustee
 ⟨3.6%⟩ Other responses included 5 from school librarian/district supervisors/a-v specialists; 16 from state library/regional consultants, and 2 from special librarians

3. Are you a member of the Library Public Relations Council? ⟨N = 370⟩
⟨9.1%⟩ Yes   ⟨87.2%⟩ No

4. Are you a member of other library or non-library public relations associations? ⟨N = 376⟩
⟨12.0%⟩ Yes   ⟨88.0%⟩ No

5. If your answer to question 4 was "yes," please list the associations: ⟨N = 31⟩

Local advertising clubs	13 responses
Regional advertising clubs	9 responses
Women in Communications	5 responses
Public Relations Society of America	3 responses
International Association of Business Communicators	1 response

6. What type of library do you work in? Please check most correct response. ⟨N = 380⟩

⟨54.2%⟩ Public library   ⟨7.6%⟩ College library
⟨9.4%⟩ Regional/system library ⟨15.6%⟩ University library
⟨0.3%⟩ Library association/   ⟨0.0%⟩ Research library
    council
⟨2.3%⟩ State library   ⟨0.3%⟩ Federal library
⟨0.8%⟩ Military base library   ⟨3.6%⟩ Special library
⟨1.8%⟩ School/instructional
    media center
⟨3.1%⟩ Other:

Academic	10 responses
Public library system	5 responses
Multi-type system	4 responses
Special	2 responses
Non-library	1 response

7. Are you the individual primarily responsible for PR in your library? ⟨N = 375⟩
⟨55.7%⟩ Yes   ⟨41.9%⟩ No

For questions 8 through 15, percentages were figured for the 232 respondents who filled in this section. Since not all questions were answered by these individuals, the "missing" percentage is also shown for each question.

8. What term is used to designate PR in your library (regarding position descriptions, budget items, etc)? Check most correct response. ⟨N = 232⟩
⟨3.4%⟩ Community services   ⟨1.3%⟩ Patron relations
⟨8.1%⟩ Public information   ⟨11.2%⟩ Publicity
⟨25.8%⟩ Public relations   ⟨5.2%⟩ Community relations
⟨39.6%⟩ Missing
⟨5.5%⟩ Other: Responses did not provide another term as such, but indicated personal opinions about the different terms used.

9. Do you spend at ⅓ of your work time on PR? ⟨N = 233⟩
⟨14.3%⟩ Yes   ⟨46.1%⟩ No   ⟨39.3%⟩ Missing

10. Do you have a written, formal job/position description? ⟨N = 109⟩
⟨28.9%⟩ Yes   ⟨25.5%⟩ No   ⟨45.6%⟩ Missing

11. How long have you been responsible for library PR in your present position? ⟨N = 220⟩
⟨9.4%⟩ Less than one year   ⟨18.5%⟩ Between 6 and 15 years
⟨27.9%⟩ Between one and five   ⟨3.1%⟩ Over fifteen years
years
⟨41.1%⟩ Missing

12. Is your present job the first job you have held in library PR? ⟨N = 212⟩
⟨25.8%⟩ Yes   ⟨29.4%⟩ No   ⟨44.8%⟩ Missing

13. If you are not the library director, to whom do you report? ⟨N = 84⟩
⟨15.4%⟩ Library director   ⟨0.5%⟩ Head of public services
⟨1.8%⟩ Assistant director   ⟨78.1⟩ Missing
⟨4.2%⟩ Other: Assortment of responses, most indicating a department head.

14. Are you the only person in your library with major PR responsibilities? ⟨N = 230⟩
⟨27.1%⟩ Yes   ⟨32.8%⟩ No   ⟨40.1%⟩ Missing

15. If others besides yourself are employed with major PR responsibilities, please provide the number(s) in the most appropriate categories below. (Include yourself in the numbers.)
Answers to this question were invalidated. Question unclear or not understood.

16. Does your library have a specific policy statement dealing with public relations? ⟨N = 379⟩
⟨8.3%⟩ Yes   ⟨90.1%⟩ No   ⟨1.6%⟩Missing

17. What is your library's current operating budget? Check below. ⟨N = 376⟩
⟨10.7%⟩ Below $100,000
⟨17.7%⟩ Between $100,000 and $249,999

⟨25.3%⟩ Between $250,000 and $749,999
⟨21.9%⟩ Between $750,000 and $1,999,999
⟨22.4%⟩ Over $2,000,000
 ⟨2.1%⟩ Missing

18. Is there a specific budget item for public relations in your library? ⟨N = 373⟩
⟨24.0%⟩ Yes　　　　　　　⟨75.2%⟩ No　　　　　　　⟨2.9%⟩ Missing

19. If your answer to question 18 was "yes," what percentage of your library's current operating budget is the PR budget? ⟨N = 71⟩

Percentage of library's budget	Responses in percents
1	7
2	4.4
3	1.8
4	1
5	1.8
6	0.8
7	5
10	0.8
17	0.3
Missing	81.5

20. If your answer to question 18 was "no," what percentage of your library's current operating budget do you estimate the PR budget to be? ⟨N = 160⟩

Percentage of library's budget	Response in percents
1	21.1
2	8.6
3	4.9
4	1.8
5	2.6
6	0.5
7	0.3
8	0.3
9	0.3
10	0.8
12	0.3
20	0.3
Missing	58.3

21. Does your library have a planned program in public relations? ⟨N = 370⟩

⟨32.6%⟩ Yes ⟨63.8%⟩ No ⟨3.6%⟩ Missing

22. How long has your library had a planned program of library PR?- ⟨N = 129⟩

⟨4.4%⟩ Less than one year ⟨8.6%⟩ Between 6 and 15 years
⟨16.1%⟩ Between one and five ⟨4.4%⟩ Over 15 years
years
⟨66.4%⟩ Missing

23. Were you responsible in helping to establish this program? ⟨N = 131⟩

⟨26%⟩ Yes ⟨8.1%⟩ No ⟨65.9%⟩Missing

24. Do you feel that you are now an important part of the continuing review and modification of this PR program? ⟨N = 130⟩

⟨29.7%⟩ Yes ⟨4.2%⟩ No ⟨66.1%⟩ Missing

25. Does your library have a Friends group or other organized major volunteer effort which provides public relations activities and support for your library? ⟨N = 370⟩

⟨54.7%⟩ Yes ⟨41.7%⟩ No ⟨3.6%⟩ Missing

26. Does your library have formally adopted written goals and objectives for library PR? ⟨N = 368⟩

⟨11.5%⟩ Yes ⟨84.4%⟩ No ⟨4.2%⟩ Missing

27. Do you think that formal library science education is necessary to be a library PR specialist? ⟨N = 366⟩

⟨22.4%⟩ Yes ⟨72.9%⟩ No ⟨4.7%⟩ Missing

28. Do you think that formal education in art, journalism, PR, mass communications, and/or other PR fields is necessary to be a library PR specialist? ⟨N = 363⟩

⟨57.8%⟩ Yes ⟨36.7%⟩ No ⟨5.5%⟩ Missing

29. What is your education and training/experience for the position you now hold? Please check the "highest" level categories below. ⟨N = 363⟩

⟨3.1%⟩ Some college-level training in library science
⟨7.0%⟩ Some college-level training in PR subjects
⟨3.4%⟩ An undergraduate major/degree in library science

⟨3.1%⟩ An undergraduate major/degree in a PR subject
⟨92.4%⟩ Graduate degree in library science
⟨1.0%⟩ Graduate degree in a PR subject
⟨5.2%⟩ Work, internship and/or practical training in library science
⟨13.8%⟩ Work, internship and/or practical training in PR fields
⟨0.3%⟩ Primarily self-taught in library science
⟨20.1%⟩ Primarily self-taught in PR skills
⟨7.0%⟩ Other: Degrees in other fields

30. Have you attended at least one workshop and/or substantive meeting on library PR in the last two years? ⟨N = 378⟩
⟨66.7%⟩ Yes   ⟨31.8%⟩ No   ⟨1.6%⟩ Missing

31. How do you rate the following possible sources for library PR ideas and help? Check most appropriate level. ⟨N = 378⟩

Sources	Little or no help	Some help	Great help
Periodicals, books, and other published materials	5.2%	59.1%	32.0%
Regional and state library staff	50.5%	34.6%	6.8%
Library associations	18.0%	64.1%	12%
Workshops on library PR	4.9%	38.3%	47.7%
Personal contact with PR "experts"	9.6%	28.6%	53.4%

32. Are most of your library's publicity pieces produced in-house? (Such as posters, announcements, radio spots, etc.) ⟨N = 376⟩
⟨88.3%⟩ Yes   ⟨9.4%⟩ No   ⟨2.4%⟩ Missing

33. If your answer to question 32 was "yes," which of the following suppliers does your library purchase from at least once a year? Check those which apply. ⟨N = 376⟩
⟨66.1%⟩ American Library Association (National Library Week)
⟨47.1%⟩ Children's Book Council
⟨29.4%⟩ Gaylord Library Supplies

⟨1.3%⟩ Jewish Book Council
⟨46.1%⟩ Upstart Library Promotionals
⟨15.6%⟩ Library Promotions

35. Does your library employ outside PR/advertising specialists to design and/or produce any of your library's publicity pieces? ⟨N = 372⟩
⟨25.5%⟩ Yes   ⟨71.4%⟩ No   ⟨3.1%⟩ Missing

36. Are you presently a member of the PR committee of any of the following? ⟨N = 135⟩
⟨1.0%⟩ Local library club
⟨5.5%⟩ Regional/system library association (within your state)
⟨8.9%⟩ State library association
⟨2.1%⟩ Regional library association
⟨16.7%⟩ National library association (Respondents may have confused this category with membership in the PR Section.)

37. Do you provide any free-lance or volunteer PR assistance to other community agencies or associations? ⟨N = 367⟩
⟨29.7%⟩ Yes   ⟨65.9%⟩ No   ⟨4.4%⟩ Missing

38. Is the library staff regularly informed about library activities and happenings? ⟨N = 376⟩
⟨95.3%⟩ Yes   ⟨2.6%⟩ No   ⟨2.1%⟩ Missing

39. What methods are used by the library administration to communicate with the library staff? Please check. ⟨N = 356⟩
⟨81.0%⟩ Administrative memoranda and announcements
⟨37.0%⟩ Staff newsletters
⟨87.0%⟩ Staff meetings
⟨20.6%⟩ Other:
       Minutes of meetings
       Bulletin board
       Grapevine/personal contact/coffee breaks/etc.
       Committee meetings

40. Is the library staff involved in planning and executing the library's PR program? ⟨N = 367⟩
⟨78.6%⟩ Yes   ⟨16.9%⟩ No   ⟨17.0%⟩ Missing

41. What methods are used by your library to discover public opinion about the library? Check all which apply. ⟨N = 322⟩

⟨61.0%⟩ User surveys
⟨26.6%⟩ Community surveys
⟨7.6%⟩ Marketing studies
⟨6.5%⟩ Analysis of mass communication
⟨86.5%⟩ Informal patron reactions
⟨60.4%⟩ Program attendance statistics
⟨63.0%⟩ Informal community contacts
⟨49.7%⟩ Formal suggestions (boxes, forms, etc.)
⟨50.8%⟩ Lay representation on boards and committees
⟨5.2%⟩ Other:
        Faculty committee/liaison
        Use-pattern analysis
        Exhibits at fairs
        Group presentation feedback

The author expresses appreciation to Bill Corbin and Julie Julian for their assistance in the preparation of this appendix.

BIBLIOGRAPHY

Following are some selected monographs for those who wish to do further reading in the fields of public relations and marketing. Additional items may be found in the "References" at the end of each chapter.

Adams, Donald. *Museum Public Relations*. Nashville, American Association for State and Local History, 1982.

Angoff, Alan, ed. *Public Relations for Libraries: Essays in Communication Techniques*. Westport, Conn., Greenwood, 1973.

Arnold, David S., Becker, Christine S. and Kellar, Elizabeth K., eds. *Effective Communication: Getting the Message Across*. Washington, D.C., International City Managers Association, 1983.

Boone, Louise E. and Kurtz, David L. *Contemporary Marketing*. 3d ed. Hinsdale, Ill., Dryden, 1980.

Cronin, Blaise, ed. *The Marketing of Library and Information Services*. London, Eng. Aslib, 1981.

Cutlip, Scott and Center, Allen. *Effective Public Relations*. 6th ed. Englewood Cliffs, N.J., Prentice-Hall, 1985.

Edsall, Marian S. *Library Promotion Handbook*. Phoenix, Ariz., Oryx, 1980.

Ford, Gary T., ed. *Marketing and the Library*. New York, Haworth, 1984. (Also published as special issue of the *Journal of Library Administration*, Vol. 4, No. 4.)

Gilbert, William. *Public Relations in Local Government*. Washington, D.C., International City Managers Association, 1975.

Kies, Cosette. *Problems in Library Public Relations*. New York, Bowker, 1974.

_____. *Projecting a Positive Image Through Public Relations*. Chicago, American Library Association/AASL, 1979.

Kotler, Philip. *Marketing for Nonprofit Organizations*. 2d ed. Englewood Cliffs, N.J., Prentice-Hall, 1982.

_____. *Marketing Management: Analysis, Planning and Control*. 5th ed. Englewood Cliffs, N.J., Prentice-Hall, 1984.

_____. *Principles of Marketing*. 2d ed. Englewood Cliffs, N.J., Prentice-Hall, 1983.

Kotler, Philip, Ferrell, O. C. and Lamb, Charles W., Jr. *Cases and Readings in Nonprofit Marketing*. 2d ed. Englewood Cliffs, N.J., Prentice-Hall, 1982.

Lesley, Philip, ed. *Lesley's Public Relations Handbook*. 2d ed. Englewood Cliffs, N.J., Prentice-Hall, 1977.

Lovelock, Christopher H. and Weinberg, Charles B. *Cases in Public and Nonprofit Marketing*. Palo Alto, Calif., The Scientific Press, 1977.

_____ and _____. *Readings in Public and Nonprofit Marketing*. Palo Alto, Calif., The Scientific Press, 1978.

Manley, Will. *Snowballs in the Book Drop*. Hamden, Conn., The Shoe String Press, 1982.

Rados, David L. *Marketing for Nonprofit Organizations*. Boston, Mass., Auburn House, 1981.

Rathmell, John M. *Marketing in the Service Sector*. Cambridge, Mass., Winthrop, 1974.

Ruffner, Robert H. *Handbook of Publicity and Public Relations for the Nonprofit Organization.* Englewood Cliffs, N.J., Prentice-Hall, 1984.

Rummel, Kathleen, ed. *Persuasive Public Relations for Libraries.* Chicago, American Library Association, 1983.

Sherman, Steve. *ABC's of Library Promotion.* 2d ed. Metuchen, N.J., Scarecrow, 1980.

Tull, Donald S. and Hawkins Del I. *Marketing Research: Measurement and Method.* 3d ed. New York, Macmillan, 1984.

Unruh, Adolph and Weller, Robert A. *Public Relations for Schools.* Belmont, Calif., Lear Sigler/Fearon, 1974.

Weingand, Darlene E., ed. *Marketing for Libraries and Information Agencies.* Norwood, N.J., Ablex, 1984.

Yale, David R: *The Publicity Handbook.* New York, Bantam, 1982.

INDEX

197